★ GAME FOR LIFE ★

TROY AIKMAN

A PRO FOOTBALL HALL OF FAME BIOGRAPHY

★ GAME FOR LIFE ★

TROY AIKMAN

A PRO FOOTBALL HALL OF FAME BIOGRAPHY

Clarence Hill Jr.

RANDOM HOUSE
NEW YORK

Copyright © 2019 by Pro Football Hall of Fame

All rights reserved. Published in the United States by
Random House Children's Books, a division of
Penguin Random House LLC, New York.

Random House and the colophon are registered
trademarks of Penguin Random House LLC.

Photographs courtesy of Pro Football Hall of Fame

Visit us on the Web! rhcbooks.com

Educators and librarians, for a variety of teaching tools,
visit us at RHTeachersLibrarians.com

Library of Congress Cataloging-in-Publication Data
Name: Hill, Clarence, Jr. author.
Title: Troy Aikman / By Clarence Hill Jr.
Description: First edition. | New York: Random House, [2019] |
Series: Game for life
Identifiers: LCCN 2018042717 | ISBN 978-1-63565-252-9 (trade
hardcover) | ISBN 978-1-9848-5219-9 (hardcover library binding) |
ISBN 978-1-63565-253-6 (ebook)
Subjects: LCSH: Aikman, Troy, 1966– —Juvenile literature. |
Quarterbacks (Football)—United States—Biography—Juvenile
literature. | Dallas Cowboys (Football team)—Juvenile literature.
Classification: LCC GV939.A46 H55 2019 | DDC 796.332092 [B]—dc23

Printed in the United States of America
10 9 8 7 6 5 4 3 2 1
First Edition

"Individual commitment to a group effort—that is what makes a team work, a company work, a society work, a civilization work."
—Vince Lombardi

CHAPTER 1

IF YOU COULD DREAM up the perfect quarterback, he would look like Troy Aikman.

A six-foot-four, 220-pound, perfectly designed prototype with Hollywood good looks. Picture a clean-shaven Chris Hemsworth, who plays Thor in the Avengers series.

Aikman enjoyed a storybook career that lived up to every expectation imaginable. After an All-American career in college at UCLA, he was picked number one overall in the 1989 NFL Draft by the most popular team in pro sports, the Dallas Cowboys.

He took them from the depths of despair to being the dominant team of the 1990s, with three Super

Bowl titles in four years. He ended his career celebrated as an all-time great with his induction into the Pro Football Hall of Fame.

From the outside looking in, Troy seemingly had it made from birth. He was the natural. He was destined for greatness and ultimately achieved it.

But the truth is not as pretty and clean as the picture.

It began with a California kid growing up dreaming of playing baseball in the major leagues. Then, at age twelve, he moved with his family to rural Oklahoma—specifically, to the small town of Henryetta, with a sprawling population of roughly six thousand.

Once there, Troy was quickly introduced to life on the farm. He was raised on hard work, responsibility, and discipline by a father—the Babe Ruth of welders—who had no time for fun and games.

"That was a lifestyle that was foreign to me," Troy later said about moving to the farm. "It helped teach me to embrace the difficult times. No one, I don't care who it is, ever goes through life and [does] not have some setbacks."

Those teachings would serve Aikman well in his roundabout route to stardom.

★ ★ ★

Football was not the first choice or childhood dream of Troy Kenneth Aikman, the youngest of three kids and the only boy born to Kenneth and Charlyn in West Covina, California.

The family soon settled in Cerritos, a suburb of Los Angeles, and Troy grew up a typical California kid. He loved to ride his bike everywhere he went and took a liking to all sports—but mainly baseball. He inherited this passion for the sport from his mother and her side of the family.

Charlyn didn't just watch baseball games. She had a scorebook and kept score while her favorite team, the California Angels, played.

"When he was little, I used to watch sports on television, but his dad wasn't into it," Charlyn said. "And, yes, I used to make my own scorebook. I started that as a kid. Baseball was my favorite."

Her brothers were big-time baseball players. One

played in college and then joined a famous traveling four-player softball team called the King and His Court. Troy's uncles' experience helped build the foundation for his affinity for the sport.

That's what he and his friends played and loved for the first twelve years of his life.

He concedes now that if he had stayed on the West Coast, he probably would have ended up playing professional baseball.

But that was before Aikman's dad decided to go against what seemed to be the American trend of chasing happiness from the East to the West. He migrated from the West Coast to the Midwest, rather than the other way around.

Kenneth, a construction foreman and a welder, had grown up in Iowa and wanted to get out of the rat race, the traffic, and the congestion in California. He longed to get back to country living. So Kenneth bought 172 acres of farmland in tiny Henryetta, Oklahoma, 1,419 miles from Cerritos. "He had a friend in California, and Henryetta was his hometown," Charlyn said. "We went there on vacation one summer, and he really liked it."

The farm was also seven miles from the nearest

town. So for Troy Aikman, it was a culture shock in every sense.

"He thought he had just watched *The Beverly Hillbillies* [a sitcom in the 1960–70s about a rural family who moved to Beverly Hills after striking it big in oil]," Troy's childhood friend Daren Lesley recalled. "He was shell-shocked, going from a solid concrete jungle to a dirt road, from not seeing many farm animals to owning them. I don't know what his chores were when he was a kid in Cerritos. But the yard got a whole lot bigger, and he had a lot of chores to tend to on the farm."

Kenneth didn't have much time for sports, and his son learned at a young age that he would have to grow up tough or he wasn't going to make it.

Kenneth built the Aikmans' house himself, with two other carpenters and his son.

They had animals—cows, horses, pigs, and chickens—that had to be fed before Troy went to school. Mountainous bales of hay had to be hauled.

"I say 'we hauled hay,'" Aikman recalled. "We cut our own hay. I hauled hay. There were nights or days where I would be hauling hay all day long, and

then I'd leave to go to an American Legion baseball game or something. . . . I'd go play in the game,
doubleheader, and I'd get back. And it was supposed
to rain, and my dad's still out in the fields getting
the hay picked up. I'm back out there till five or six
in the morning, making sure all the hay is in."

Kenneth was not the sympathetic or soft sort. He
once cut off the tip of his finger while working but
never stopped or took a break to tend to it. He was
tough, and he raised his son to be tough through
hard work.

There was no getting away from it.

In one of his few interviews, Kenneth told the
Fort Worth Star-Telegram he never showed Troy
much affection.

And Troy certainly noticed. But he also appreciated the tough love.

Troy says his father demanded a lot, and there
were certainly consequences for poor decisions.
But this experience likely set the foundation for
the discipline and responsibility and toughness
that would serve him well as quarterback of America's team.

"At a young age, it was 'do what you were told to

do,' and if he needed help doing something, he expected you to do it," Aikman recalled.

One story he will never forget is from the summer when he was fourteen. "My dad came driving in ... and he says, 'Hey, I got you a summer job.' And I said, 'Well, okay. What is it?' And he says, 'You're going to weld.' And I said, 'I've never welded in my life.' He says, 'It's okay. You're going to go audition right now.'"

So Troy and his father got in the truck and headed to the job. He told Troy to do exactly what he said.

"I'd been around him, seen him weld, but I've never done it," Troy said. "But we go over, and I've got the hood on, the welding hood, and he's in my ear, telling me what to do. . . . And after I'm done, he says, 'Okay, now brush the weld.' I brushed the weld, and the guy came over and checked the weld, and he hired me. I welded that whole summer.

"That was kind of the way he did things."

But the move to Oklahoma also set his sports life in a new and focused direction.

Because the family moved from California in the summer, Troy didn't get to make friends until the fall, when he signed up for football at his dad's urging.

"I wasn't going to play, but football was his favorite sport," Troy said. "If he hadn't said anything, I'm convinced I wouldn't have played football that year, probably would not have played football again. Not wanting to disappoint him, I went down . . . and signed up."

Aikman had played football, baseball, and basketball on youth teams in California. He was always bigger, faster, and stronger than most of the boys his age. And most of the time in youth football, the best athlete plays quarterback.

But when he got to Henryetta, interestingly, he told the coaches he was a fullback/tight end, Daren Lesley recalled with a laugh. Troy apparently didn't know how he would fit in.

It didn't take too long for them to figure out he was a quarterback.

After a few games at fullback, getting his head knocked in, Aikman was ready to go back to quarterback as well.

Again, Troy was a natural. He became a three-sport star in football, basketball, and baseball.

Football grew to be his focus because it was almost a religion in Oklahoma, especially in small towns. He was All-State and wanted to play football in college, although he was good enough at baseball to receive draft interest from the New York Mets.

Knowing that, you probably think Troy Aikman won every sports trophy or medal possible in high school. State champions in football? Nope. Baseball? No. In fact, the only state medal Troy ever won in high school was for typing.

A typical teenage boy, Troy decided to take typing as a sophomore because there were a lot of girls in the class, according to Daren Lesley. Charlyn backed up that version of the story. But Troy became so proficient that he continued to take typing.

His sister Tammy was in the class and was the best typist in the school, but she couldn't go to the state typing competition. It conflicted with a softball game.

So Troy Aikman won state in typing.

"It was ridiculous for a stud athlete and quarterback to do it," Lesley said. "He typed ninety-four words a minute. He was so good at it. In class, he would be typing and hitting my return in between sentences. He would have done both our assignments while he was messing with me.

"One [time] we had a manuscript to do, and we had ten days to do it. He was done on the third day. I got done with thirty minutes to spare on the last day. And when I turned my paper in, with Wite-Out all over it, [the teacher] said, 'Daren, you handed this in a week ago.' He had done both of them and never told me."

That was it for Troy as far as titles and individual success at Henryetta. It was the smallest school in the smallest classification in Oklahoma. The football team went 6–4 his senior season, which was pretty good for Henryetta. It was the first time in twenty-five years that Henryetta finished with a winning record.

And his big-league talent was obvious. After a game, an opposing coach even told him, "We'll be watching you someday on *Monday Night Football*."

CHAPTER 2

AFTER AIKMAN'S LAST SEASON of high school football, the college recruitment battle began.

Both the University of Oklahoma and Oklahoma State wanted him. It was a competition between legendary Sooners coach Barry Switzer and then up-and-coming Oklahoma State coach Jimmy Johnson, who would later become Aikman's first coach with the Cowboys.

Aikman initially committed to Oklahoma State and Johnson because he envisioned playing both football and baseball in college. He could do that there, while at the University of Oklahoma, Sooners football was king.

Still, Aikman promised the Sooners he would give them a final visit. The trip wasn't supposed to be a big deal. He was so firmly committed to Oklahoma State that he didn't even ask his parents to go with him.

But once he got there, Switzer and the Sooners pulled out all the stops, wowing Aikman with the school's rich history, tradition, and championships. Troy hadn't won much at Henryetta, and Oklahoma State couldn't back up the promise of winning with the history of doing so. Switzer had also switched his offensive scheme from a run-oriented, option attack and promised to pass more if Troy came to the University of Oklahoma.

"He went on a Friday," Charlyn recalled. "Saturday morning, he woke us and said, 'I need you to come.' We went, of course. He decided he liked what he saw, and he wanted to go there. I met with Barry Switzer, and I asked him about the offense. Everybody knew OU [liked to run the ball]. He said, 'We are going to pass.' I said that was fine, then. It was tough breaking it to Jimmy."

★ ★ ★

The decision to choose Oklahoma had to survive one final appeal from the New York Mets.

Aikman knew he wanted to play football in college, because it gave him his best chance of going pro. Yet he would have liked to one day tell people he'd gotten drafted in baseball, his first love.

The Mets pushed hard and kept pressing him for an answer.

"I just wouldn't answer. Finally, the draft director called me and said, 'Look, we have to know what it will take to sign you, because we're not going to waste a pick.' And I think I told him, you know, a hundred thousand dollars or two hundred thousand, and he said, 'Two hundred thousand!' Darryl Strawberry at the time was their biggest threat. They said, 'Darryl Strawberry doesn't even make two hundred thousand dollars.' And I said, 'Well, that's what it's going to take if you want me.' And so the guy said, 'Well, you have a nice career in Oklahoma.'"

If only that were the case.

★ ★ ★

Here is where the story changed, and things got a little murky.

According to Troy, the Sooners switched their offense from a wishbone-option attack, with three backs behind the quarterback, to the I formation for running back Marcus Dupree when Troy was a senior in high school. But Barry Switzer told him they were going to stay in it when he came to Oklahoma, except for his freshman year.

Dupree transferred.

And the quarterback who was going to start Aikman's freshman year was more suited for the wishbone attack.

★ WISHBONE FORMATION ★

When Troy Aikman picked the University of Oklahoma, it had the appearance of a fish-out-of-water story from the beginning.

Aikman was athletic, but he was not a running quarterback. He was built in the mold of the classic drop-back passer, the kind that NFL teams covet.

But at Oklahoma, he was an odd fit, because the Sooners were a run-oriented team. Coach Barry Switzer featured the wishbone offense, which required the quarterback to run the triple-option attack.

It had three backs—a fullback and two halfbacks—line up behind the quarterback.

In the wishbone, the quarterback either fakes or hands the ball to the fullback, who dives between the guard and tackle on either side. If the quarterback keeps the ball, he can sprint to the side and pitch the ball to a trailing halfback or keep it, depending on the reaction of the defensive player.

The quarterback is the key. He has to decide quickly on each play while running at full speed.

It's similar to the zone read or read option that is used in today's college game. Tim Tebow won the Heisman Trophy and two national titles at the University of Florida running the zone read. Vince Young, at the University of Texas, and Cam Newton, at Auburn, won national titles doing the same. It's an offense for running quarterbacks.

Aikman's strength was passing, not running. He was a prototypical drop-back passer, meaning that he would get the football from the center and step back to make a pass. That is why Charlyn was so concerned about the kind of offense Switzer planned to run at the University of Oklahoma.

But Jamelle Holieway, who joined the team when Troy was a sophomore, was the perfect wishbone quarterback. The five-foot-nine, 185-pound QB was quick and shifty. He was slick with the football. He made smart, decisive calls about when to hand off and when to keep it.

Switzer has called him the best wishbone quarterback in Oklahoma history.

Said Holieway: "It's something I'm proud of. I know that in our type of offense, we're not a passing team. We go with what we do best."

It proved to be best for Holieway and Oklahoma, and best for Aikman, too.

> The 1985 national title was the third and last for Switzer at Oklahoma running the wishbone.
>
> Aikman transferred to UCLA, where he found an offense that fit his skills. And the rest is history. The three Super Bowl titles and the Hall of Fame might never have come if he had stayed at Oklahoma as a square peg in a round hole.

"'Next year, we're going to go back to the wishbone, because it's what our players are best suited for,'" Troy recalled Switzer telling him when he was recruiting him. "'But then, when you're ready to play, we're going to go back to the pro-style offense.'"

That's what he told Troy and tight end Keith Jackson.

But apparently, a different story was being told to some other recruits in the class.

"These other running backs, like Patrick Collins out of Tulsa and Lydell Carr, who was one of the top recruits in the country, he was telling them they were going to stay in the wishbone," Troy said. "But none of us were talking to each other.... Half my class signed thinking they're going to . . . stay in the wishbone; the other half signed thinking they're going to go to a pro-style offense."

So Troy redshirted his freshman season—he delayed playing for a year so he could extend his eligibility. Then, going into his sophomore season, he was ready to start. But instead of going back to the I formation, or a more pro-style passing offense, as promised, Switzer decided to alter the wishbone with some pass elements that Oklahoma learned from the Air Force Academy.

"I couldn't run the real triple-option threat. They tried to change it," Troy said. "I should not have been running the wishbone."

Still, Troy did well enough to lead the Sooners to victories in their first three games, though they were no offensive powerhouse.

But in the fourth game, against the Miami Hurricanes, he appeared to be finally getting in a rhythm. Troy completed six of his first seven passes for 131 yards and a touchdown. Then he broke his leg, and Oklahoma lost, 27–14. That season, he had completed twenty-seven of forty-seven passes for 442 yards and a touchdown.

But Jamelle Holieway, who was the prototypical wishbone quarterback and arguably the best in Sooners history, took over the next week, and the offense began to hum. Oklahoma didn't lose again. They won their next five games by a combined score of 216–33, en route to the national championship.

★ ★ ★

Troy's career at Oklahoma seemed to be over, but he had already been thinking about transferring as soon as the injury occurred.

Before the Miami game, the offensive coordinator had planted a seed in Aikman's head about his status on the team, despite the 3–0 start.

"'Hey,' he says, 'I just want to give you a heads-up. I don't want you to get upset, but at some point in the game, we may pull you and put Jamelle Holieway in,'" Troy recalled. "I said, 'What do you mean? I'm not supposed to get upset about that? You tell me right before kickoff.' Well, I went out and was lighting it up. That's when I broke my leg. And Barry always says, 'Hey, we [still] would've won the national championship if Troy hadn't got hurt. He would've been player of the year.' But no, I wasn't. They were getting ready to bench me! They told me before the game!"

Troy laughs about it now. He said it worked out best for both sides. "I loved OU, but I just was not happy . . . as a player," Troy said. "So I started kind of putting some feelers out there around the country, different places that I was interested in, to see if there was any interest in me. I was getting word back that there would be some interest, and then spring ball started. They told me it was an open competition."

Some open competition. The Sooners had just won a national championship with a true freshman quarterback who had won offensive player of the year in the conference.

Troy went through the farce of a competition for about a week and then told offensive coordinator Jim Donnan that he wanted to transfer. Donnan said they had to break the news to Barry Switzer. So they reluctantly went down to Switzer's office.

Troy told him he wanted to transfer, and it seemingly lifted a weight off Barry Switzer.

"He goes, 'Man, I think that's great!'" Troy said

with a laugh. "He says, 'What schools do you want to go to?' You know, he couldn't . . . get on the phone fast enough with some of these schools. But he was helpful. I think that deep down—we've never really talked about it—but I think deep down Barry felt bad. I think he knew I was in the wrong place. He knew that when he recruited me. Maybe he recruited me just to keep me from going to Oklahoma State. I do think he felt bad about my situation, being at the wrong school, and wanted to help me any way he could."

Troy narrowed his list of schools to UCLA, Arizona State, and Miami, where Jimmy Johnson had gone from Oklahoma State.

CHAPTER 3

SWITZER WAS HELPFUL. He called coach Terry Donahue at UCLA to let him know Aikman was available to transfer there.

"We contacted UCLA for Troy," Switzer told reporters at the time. "I talked to Terry Donahue, and he's interested in having Troy."

It was the perfect fit for Aikman on the field. "I wanted to go somewhere where I could throw the ball and do what I do best," he said.

It was also perfect off the field, since he got to go back to California. Unfortunately, it also meant turning Jimmy Johnson down a second time—first at Oklahoma State and now at Miami. But being in

California, back near family and friends from his childhood, and living the West Coast lifestyle were worth it.

"It felt good to be back on the West Coast, and Coach Donahue, to this day, I mean, he just was someone that I have so much respect for," Troy said. "I don't hold anyone really in higher regard than him. It was just ... a really good fit for me all the way around. I liked that football wasn't the most important thing on campus. You know? I really enjoyed that. It's such a different atmosphere than what Oklahoma had been.... Those were probably the best years of my life; certainly the last two years that I played ... were some of my fondest years ever."

After sitting out a season, per the NCAA transfer rules, Troy began his career as a UCLA Bruin in 1987 and became an immediate success—to the delight of Bruins fans everywhere. They couldn't believe someone with so much talent had simply been given away.

Again, Troy was the prototype of a quarterback, with a rocket arm. He was not suited to play in the wishbone-option offense at Oklahoma, but he was a godsend in UCLA's pro-style passing attack. His smarts and field vision, as well as the work ethic instilled in him in Henryetta, won over his new teammates.

At first, his UCLA teammates teased the city boy turned country boy who was now back in the city. They jokingly called him Bocephus (the nickname of Hank Williams Jr., one of Troy's favorite country singers). But they found out that no one worked harder and was more committed to winning than their new quarterback. Aikman was always the last to leave the practice field and the meeting room after poring over film. And he became an immediate hit at UCLA.

It didn't take long for him to be considered one of the best quarterbacks in the nation.

"Barry Switzer told me he was good," said UCLA coach Terry Donahue, "but he didn't tell me he was *that* good."

Aikman led the nation in passing efficiency and was named the Pac-10 Conference offensive player of the year in his first season.

But he will always have one bad memory, a 17–13

loss to cross-town rival USC after leading 13–0 at halftime. It was his only bad game of the season. He completed just eleven of twenty-six passes for 171 yards while throwing three interceptions. He hadn't thrown three interceptions in the first ten games combined.

"That wasn't my best game," Aikman said.

Aikman and UCLA finished the season with a 20–16 victory over the Florida Gators in the Aloha Bowl. Aikman was named one of the game's most outstanding players, along with a freshman running back at Florida named Emmitt Smith, who rushed for 128 yards in the game. It was the first meeting of two players who would later be teammates on the Dallas Cowboys, as back-to-back first-round picks in 1989 and 1990.

But first they would head into the 1988 season as leading candidates for the Heisman Trophy. And things looked good for Aikman early as the Bruins opened the season winning their first six games—including a statement-making blowout of the University of Nebraska Cornhuskers in the second game of the season. Aikman threw for three touchdowns on eleven-of-fourteen passing as UCLA led, 38–13, in the first half. After some meaningless points by Nebraska late in the game, UCLA finished with a 41–28 win.

The Bruins would lose to Washington State and then again to cross-town rival USC to finish 10–2 for the second straight year with Aikman.

Aikman won the 1988 Davey O'Brien Award as the nation's top quarterback, the first in UCLA history. He finished third in the Heisman Trophy race, with a running back from Oklahoma State named Barry Sanders taking top honors. A few months later, Sanders would be selected third behind the top pick Aikman in the 1989 NFL Draft.

Aikman, who finished his college career as number two in career passing in UCLA history despite playing only two years there, was elected to the College Football Hall of Fame in 2008. UCLA retired his number 8 jersey in 2014.

"Troy is the embodiment of what it means to be a Bruin," UCLA athletic director Dan Guerrero said in announcing the jersey retirement. "He was a leader both on and off the field at UCLA and with the Dallas Cowboys while setting records and establishing a lofty standard of excellence for both teams. Most admirably, and importantly, he has been an inspiration to countless people across all walks of life with the extensive work he has done in the community and with his pursuit, and ultimate completion, of a UCLA degree. We cannot think of a person more deserving of this tremendous honor than Troy."

CHAPTER 4

TROY AIKMAN'S BIGGEST REGRETS in college were never winning a Pac-10 title and never beating cross-town rival USC.

Although he finished third in the Heisman race, there was never any doubt that Troy would be the number one pick in the 1989 NFL Draft.

"Being number one was important to me. It meant a lot," he said.

Late in the season, it had come down to a battle for last place in the NFL—and thus the first pick in the draft—between the Green Bay Packers and the Dallas Cowboys.

The Cowboys got the top pick because they lost

their final game of the season to finish 3–13, while the Packers (4–12) won theirs.

And it all came full circle when Troy was preparing for his final game in college: the Cotton Bowl, against the University of Arkansas, in Dallas.

UCLA practiced for the game at Texas Stadium, home of the Cowboys. Legendary coach Tom Landry, general manager Tex Schramm, and chief scout Gil Brandt made it a point to inspect him up close and in person.

The pressure to perform was intense.

Everybody knew the Cowboys were eyeing him. The local media in Dallas made it bigger than the game.

Growing up in Oklahoma, Aikman had been a Cowboys fan. He'd idolized Coach Landry and legendary Hall of Fame quarterback Roger Staubach. So in practice, Troy felt the pressure.

"I remember that one practice I was terrible," Troy said. "I threw about five interceptions in practice. And Coach Donahue was really worried. He thought that I had too much pressure on me and it was starting to get to me. . . . I get a call the next morning, and it's Gil Brandt. He said, 'Hey, Troy, I just want you to know that I don't care if you throw seven interceptions in this game this week. You're going to be our guy. We're taking you.'"

Brandt had already been convinced while scouting Aikman earlier in the season. And Landry agreed after watching him practice during the week leading up to the Cotton Bowl.

"As we walked away from practice, Coach Landry leaned into me and said quietly, 'I've seen enough. No more practices are necessary.' That was Coach Landry's way of saying he will be our pick," Brandt wrote for the Pro Football Hall of Fame.

He would have been Landry's pick . . . if he were still coaching the Cowboys, that is. But on February 25, 1989, a brash Arkansas oil and gas tycoon named Jerry Jones bought the Cowboys for a record $140 million. He immediately fired Landry, the only coach the Cowboys had ever had in the twenty-nine-year history of the team, and hired Jimmy Johnson as head coach. Yes, the same Jimmy Johnson who had tried to recruit Aikman twice.

Johnson was Jones's former college teammate at the University of Arkansas. While Landry was revered and respected for his ability to coach, as well as his dignified demeanor, Johnson was considered a brash, cutthroat soldier of fortune who would win at all costs.

Jones was not the modest sort, either. He said he was going to run everything from socks to jocks. And he called Johnson the finest coach in America.

"What Jimmy Johnson will bring to us is worth more than if we had five Heisman Trophy winners," Jones said in his opening news conference. "History will show that one of the finest things that ever happened to the Cowboys is Jimmy Johnson."

That would one day prove to be true. But in the meantime, it caused a brutal backlash because of the way Landry was tossed aside. The Cowboys were in the midst of a downturn, with records of 7–9, 7–8, and 3–13 in 1986, 1987, and 1988, respectively. But Landry had built the franchise from scratch. He was the main reason the Cowboys were known as America's team. He was as popular as they were. He'd won two Super Bowl titles, made five Super Bowl appearances, and led the team to twenty straight winning seasons from 1966 to 1985.

This was the backdrop Troy found himself in.

He was also not sure how Jimmy would receive him after he'd turned down Johnson's offers at Oklahoma State and then at Miami.

But Johnson took a scouting trip with Brandt for a private workout with Troy and was soon convinced. Johnson told Brandt, "If we had him at Miami, we would have been 24-0 [in 1987–88] and won every game by fifty points."

The final hurdle was Jones, but that was more about the money than the pick.

Troy hired Leigh Steinberg as his agent, and they began a game of chicken with Jones, who threatened to take offensive tackle Tony Mandarich as the top pick instead of Aikman.

The 1989 NFL Draft will go down in history as one of the most talented drafts ever.

The first five picks were Troy Aikman, Tony Mandarich to the Green Bay Packers, Barry Sanders to the Detroit Lions, Derrick Thomas to the Kansas City Chiefs, and Deion Sanders to the Atlanta Falcons.

All but Mandarich are in the Pro Football Hall of Fame. Mandarich is considered one of the biggest draft disappointments in NFL history.

The entire threat by Jones was laughable for Troy and Steinberg, considering that the Cowboys were coming off a 3–13 season, losing money, and not filling up the stadium as they once had.

Steinberg said, "You won't take Tony Mandarich. You think Tony Mandarich's going to put butts in the seats?"

And then Jones resorted to a different tactic. He told Troy he should take half the salary he was asking for to play for the Cowboys because of the history, tradition, and popularity of the franchise.

"I said, 'Dallas Cowboys, they're the worst team in football . . . and you want me to take half. It should be double,'" Troy said, laughing.

Troy was Kenneth's son. He might have grown up in a small town, but he was raised on hard work and toughness.

He was no pushover.

Jones was ever the salesman, but he had taken a huge hit to his image when he fired Landry in such a careless way. He was not going to make the mistake of passing on a quarterback considered the best college prospect for the NFL since Hall of Famer John Elway.

The drama ended three days before the 1989 NFL Draft, when the Cowboys signed Troy Aikman to a six-year, $11.2 million contract, which was then the largest deal for a rookie in NFL history.

Troy was the jewel of the draft class that would become the foundation of three title teams to come.

★ THE 1989 DRAFT ★

Troy Aikman will always be remembered as the prize of the 1989 NFL Draft, one of the greatest in league history.

Aikman was one of four members of the top five players selected who ended up in the Pro Football Hall of Fame.

Aikman, of course, went first overall to the Dallas Cowboys.

The Detroit Lions took future Hall of Fame

running back Barry Sanders third. The Kansas City Chiefs took linebacker Derrick Thomas fourth, and the Atlanta Falcons took cornerback Deion Sanders fifth.

All ended up in the Hall of Fame and were considered at one time during their careers the best at what they did in the NFL.

The omission from the top five was offensive tackle Tony Mandarich, who was selected second overall by the Green Bay Packers. This is the same Mandarich whom Cowboys owner Jerry Jones had threatened to draft first if Aikman and agent Leigh Steinberg didn't agree to his contract terms.

It's all so laughable now.

Not only did Mandarich not make the Hall of Fame, but he is considered the biggest draft disappointment in NFL history.

After signing one of the richest contracts for an offensive lineman in NFL history, he lasted just three years with the Packers. His career was derailed by an addiction to painkillers and performance-enhancing drugs called steroids.

The Packers could have had Sanders or Thomas or the other Sanders.

But they chose Mandarich because of the hype, the lies, and the con job.

In 1989, *Sports Illustrated* featured Mandarich on its predraft cover, calling him the Incredible Bulk. At six-foot-five, 320 pounds, he looked and played the part of a football superhero. His coach at Michigan State, George Perles, predicted he would be the best offensive tackle ever.

So it was not folly for the Cowboys to consider him as a choice, but they needed a quarterback, and there was no denying that Aikman was the best in the land.

Mandarich built his hype and prospects by taking steroids in college and then quitting when he got to the NFL because of more stringent testing. That proved to be his downfall.

But as far as the rest of the top five, everyone got it right.

What more can be said about Aikman?

He lived up to his draft billing and hype as much as anyone else in NFL history.

Drafted first overall to be the franchise quarterback and linchpin to a rebuilding project, Aikman took the Cowboys to the first of three Super Bowl titles in his fourth year.

He was the winningest starting quarterback of the 1990s, with ninety victories in the decade. He retired with forty-seven team passing records and six trips to the Pro Bowl as well as a Super Bowl most valuable player award after the first title.

That 52–17 victory over the Buffalo Bills in Super Bowl XXVII at the Rose Bowl in Pasadena, California, where Aikman had played in college at UCLA, was his crowning achievement. Aikman completed twenty-two of thirty passes for 273 yards and four touchdowns.

"I have a real hard time classifying anything as my biggest moment, my favorite color," he's said. "I'd have to say, though, that the Super Bowl was my greatest moment in sports, and it was also my most emotional moment."

Barry Sanders will go down as one of the most electrifying runners in NFL history, if not the greatest. He certainly would have had a shot to be considered the latter if he had not retired after ten seasons, in the prime of his career. At the time of his retirement, he had the second-most rushing yards in NFL history—15,269—behind Walter Payton.

But Barry Sanders walked away, allowing Aikman's teammate Emmitt Smith to be crowned the NFL's all-time rushing king.

"I never valued it [the career rushing record] so much that I thought it was worth my dignity or Walter's dignity to pursue it amid so much media and marketing attention," said Barry, who was not fond of attention or fanfare.

There was no question who was the most breathtaking runner and who struck the most fear in the hearts of defenders from 1989 to 1998. The five-foot-nine running back was quick and elusive, and he could stop on a dime and change directions.

"He makes you miss so bad, you kind of look up in the stands and wonder if anybody's looking at you," Atlanta Falcons cornerback D. J. Johnson once remarked. "You've got sixty thousand people in there and you wonder if anyone saw you miss that tackle."

Barry Sanders was the first back to rush for more than one thousand yards in his first ten NFL seasons.

He was also the third to top two thousand in a season when he set a league record with 2,053 in 1997. He earned NFL MVP honors that season. He also won four rushing titles during his career and was first- or second-team All-Pro for ten straight years.

Derrick Thomas was arguably the greatest player to ever play for the Kansas City Chiefs. Legendary NFL scout Gil Brandt considers him the second-best rushing linebacker of all time, behind Hall of Famer Lawrence Taylor.

Thomas was the fourth player drafted in 1989, after a standout career at Alabama. He was a star from the outset. He had ten sacks as a rookie and was named the NFL defensive rookie of the year.

In 1990, he set an NFL record with seven sacks in a game against the Seattle Seahawks en route to leading the league with twenty sacks on the season.

It began the first of nine consecutive trips to the Pro Bowl.

"Derrick was one of those rare players—there aren't many—that an offense has to be aware of every time the ball is snapped," said Gunther Cunningham, who was either defensive coordinator or head coach for most of Thomas's eleven seasons in Kansas City.

"Athletically, he simply overmatched just about every guy he went against. He had the quickness to get around you and the strength to overpower you. That combination is hard to find," Cunningham added.

At six-foot-three and 243 pounds, Thomas was fast around the edge but also strong to bull-rush his way to the quarterback. And nobody did it better during the 1990s. His 116.5 sacks were the most in the 1990s. He also forced forty-five fumbles and had nineteen fumble recoveries.

He enjoyed everything about getting after the quarterback—the sack and the forced fumble. It was what he lived for.

"To me, a sack could be described as a play with a plot. You have ups and downs, and then all of a sudden, it's drawing to the conclusion, everybody is in suspense, it's building, and building, and boom, you have a hero," Thomas said.

He finished his career with 126.5 sacks. He

would have had more, but his life was tragically cut short following an automobile accident after the 1999 NFL regular season.

Thomas's impact on the Chiefs and the city was huge. Before his arrival in 1989, Kansas City had enjoyed just one trip to the playoffs since 1971. During his eleven-year career, the Chiefs made seven playoff appearances and won three division titles.

"He put his mark on Kansas City Chiefs football like very few players have," Chiefs founder Lamar Hunt said at Thomas's posthumous induction into the Chiefs Hall of Fame in 2001.

Deion "Prime Time" Sanders started his career as Aikman's draft mate and eventually ended up as his teammate on the 1995 Dallas Cowboys Super Bowl title team.

He, too, was great from the beginning, as predicted and expected. Deion was taken fifth by the Atlanta Falcons out of Florida State, where he was a shutdown cornerback and an electrifying kick returner.

Fittingly, in his NFL debut with the Falcons, he returned a punt sixty-eight yards for a touchdown.

Over fourteen years and 188 games in the NFL, he played with five teams, including the Falcons, San Francisco 49ers, Cowboys, Washington Redskins, and Baltimore Ravens. He also played Major League Baseball with the Atlanta Braves, Cincinnati Reds, New York Yankees, and San Francisco Giants.

He was a two-sport star who played offense and defense and special teams in the NFL. When he wasn't returning kicks or playing defense, he was used as a game-breaking wide receiver.

He was named to the All-Decade team of the 1990s as both a cornerback and punt returner.

During his career, Deion Sanders scored six touchdowns on punt returns, three on kickoff returns, and nine on interception returns. He also returned one fumble for a TD and had sixty receptions for 784 yards and three TDs during his career.

But his calling card was at cornerback, where he is considered the best cover corner in NFL history. He recorded fifty-three interceptions.

Deion retired second all-time in interception return yardage (1,331) and tied for second for most interceptions returned for a touchdown in a career (nine) and a season (three). The pinnacle came in 1994 with the 49ers, when he returned three picks for touchdowns (seventy-four, ninety-three, and ninety yards) that season, becoming the first player to have two ninety-yard interception returns for touchdowns in the same season. He was named the NFL's defensive player of the year.

He proved to be the difference in the 49ers' unseating of the defending Super Bowl champion Cowboys and going on to win the Super Bowl.

The following season, he signed with the Cowboys as a free agent and turned out to be the missing link to their third and final Super Bowl title team in 1995.

That Cowboys team already included future Hall of Famers in quarterback Troy Aikman, running back Emmitt Smith, and receiver Michael Irvin.

"We had some great players on that team," owner Jerry Jones said. "Before we signed Deion ... [I] went through every detail of his contract on a big chalkboard in front of the entire team and showed them exactly what he was going to get paid.

"When I was through, I said, 'Now, do we want him or not?' I looked and it was almost an absolutely unanimous cheer saying, 'We want him. Let's go get him.' He was a big difference-maker when we won the Super Bowl."

So those top five 1989 draft picks save for Mandarich were special.

Add in running back Eric Metcalf, who went thirteenth to the Cleveland Browns; receiver

Andre Rison, twenty-second to the Indianapolis Colts; and safety Steve Atwater, twentieth to the Denver Broncos, and this might have been the best first round in NFL history.

Of course, it all started with Aikman, the man from Henryetta, Oklahoma.

★ ★ ★

Johnson became known as a shrewd evaluator of talent and an expert at wheeling and dealing during the draft.

Four of his first six picks in 1989 were Aikman, fullback Daryl Johnston, center Mark Stepnoski, and defensive end Tony Tolbert. Along with Troy, Johnston and Tolbert won three Super Bowl titles in Dallas. Stepnoski also helped get things going as a starter along with the other three on the 1992 and 1993 Super Bowl title teams.

The glory came.

But the soap opera was just beginning for the kid from Henryetta.

★ ★ ★

Picking Troy number one overall should have satisfied the Cowboys' needs at quarterback. However, Johnson selected Steve Walsh, his former quarterback at Miami, with a first-round pick in the NFL's supplemental draft a few months later. That move muddied the waters.

The supplemental draft is held every year after the regular draft. It is for prospects who did not enter the regular draft but wanted to submit their names to play in the NFL right away, either because of grades or early graduation.

Walsh had a 23–1 record in two seasons under Johnson and had led Miami to a national championship in 1987. That was largely due to the immense talent around him. He was not in the same class of pro prospect that Troy was.

Johnson allegedly drafted Walsh to create competition at the position as possible trade bait, though he initially denied it publicly.

"We did not make this pick thinking trade," Johnson said at the time. "I think people have found out in this league, you have to have more than one quarterback. I would have kicked myself for a long time if I had passed on a player of the quality of Steve Walsh."

It brought about an air of mistrust from Troy. He felt that Walsh was the favorite of the coach because of their prior relationship.

Jones had prepared Troy for the possibility of the Cowboys' taking a quarterback in the supplemental draft. He said it was likely going to be Timm Rosenbach out of Washington State.

Troy knew Timm and wasn't bothered by it.

But when the news came of the decision to take Walsh, more than a few eyebrows were raised among Troy's close-knit group.

"I was thinking, 'Well, that's not what they told me,'" Troy said. "And he won a national championship with Jimmy. You know, and then the whole thing, everything, changed immediately."

It deepened the distrust that had already begun because of Troy's opinion of the way Johnson had run things in Miami. Johnson was 52–9 at Miami, having won the 1987 national title, led by Walsh. But the team was perceived as an outlaw program because of its flashy play, constant trash talk, and penchant for running up the score.

The situation with Walsh only fueled that perception with Troy.

"If you had anything to do with the University of Miami, I was not a fan," Troy said. "Staff, players, anyone from Miami, I didn't want anything to do with it. So it . . . got Jim and [me] off to a pretty tough start. And it lasted for a while."

It certainly wasn't the ideal way for this retooled version of America's team to get off to a good start. They had a new quarterback, a new coach, and a new owner. Now the man everything was supposed to be built around perceived that the underdog quarterback was the coach's pet.

Appearances aside, once the Cowboys got to training camp and started practicing, it was clear to all assembled that Aikman was the superior quarterback. The problem was that Johnson had stacked his coaching staff with people who had worked for him at Miami. And they all were familiar with Walsh from his success there.

But even more troubling for Aikman was the

team the Cowboys had assembled. He said his squad at UCLA had had more talent than the 1989 Cowboys.

This new quarterback, new coach, and new owner falsely believed they would come in and take the league by storm. It proved to be an overwhelming task.

They won three of their four preseason games, which fueled a false sense of achievement. That quickly came crashing down in a 28–0 blowout loss in the season opener.

The Cowboys went 1–15 in 1989. Aikman was 0–11 in the games he started. He was beaten up constantly and missed five games because of injuries. The only game the Cowboys won came against the rival Washington Redskins, with Walsh leading the way.

"We're going to have a lot of wins over the next so many years in Dallas," said Johnson after the game. "It's just good to get it started."

Along the way, Johnson and Jones found out how far away they were from truly competing for a Super Bowl championship. The Cowboys had gone

3–13 the year before the new quarterback and coach arrived. Johnson had gotten rid of many of the veteran holdovers and started fresh with a franchise quarterback in Troy Aikman.

Yet they were even worse in 1989, with a 1–15 mark.

The Cowboys needed to do something big to close the talent gap between themselves and the rest of the NFL.

Call it the Great Train Robbery.

CHAPTER 5

AFTER STARTING 0–4 IN 1989, Johnson was desperate to make something happen. He knew the Cowboys needed a miracle.

There weren't a lot of established or budding stars in the depleted roster. Of note there was only receiver Michael Irvin, a first-round pick from the 1988 draft; the 1989 draft picks, including Aikman; and superstar running back Herschel Walker.

Johnson felt the Cowboys needed a bold and blockbuster move to improve the talent on the team. He initially thought about trading Irvin but was quickly talked out of the deal because of the need to have a great receiver to catch passes from Troy, his prize rookie quarterback.

Walker, the former Heisman Trophy winner from Georgia, who had joined the Cowboys in 1986 and become an immediate star after three spectacular seasons in the United States Football League (USFL), was chosen to be offered up as trade bait. When the Cowboys had finished 3–13 in 1988, Walker was still the best offensive talent in the league. He rushed for 1,514 yards and had an additional 505 yards receiving.

He immediately drew the interest of a number of teams, including the Atlanta Falcons, who wanted to bring the greatest college football player in the history of Georgia back home.

The Cleveland Browns offered two first-round picks and their second-round picks for Walker.

But Johnson and Jones felt they could get more.

That's when the Minnesota Vikings and general manager Mike Lynn entered the picture.

Lynn thought the Vikings were just a running back away from having a Super Bowl team.

Jones and Johnson told him about the Browns'

offer but insisted they wanted current players, draft picks, and the option to get more picks if they cut the players they traded for.

Lynn fell for the bait. On October 12, 1989, he agreed to the most lopsided trade in NFL history. It ultimately included eighteen players and picks.

The Vikings got Walker, plus third-, fifth-, and tenth-round picks in the 1990 NFL Draft. They also got a third-round pick in the 1991 draft.

The Cowboys got five Vikings: linebacker Jesse Solomon, linebacker David Howard, cornerback Ike Holt, running back Darrin Nelson, and defensive end Alex Stewart.

They also received the Vikings' first-round pick in 1990, which was used to take future Hall of Fame running back Emmitt Smith.

They got the Vikings' second- and sixth-round picks in 1990.

They got the Vikings' first- and second-round picks in 1991.

They got the Vikings' second- and third-round picks in 1992 and the first-round pick in 1993.

The only player the Cowboys kept was Holt.

They had planned all along to stockpile picks to fill their roster with young college talent, further laying the foundation for the dynasty of the 1990s.

Besides Smith, among the players the Cowboys got as draft picks were receiver Alvin Harper, defensive tackle Russell Maryland, cornerback Kevin Smith, safety Darren Woodson, and linebacker Dixon Edwards.

The Cowboys also added more talent through free agency. Most notably, the team acquired tight end Jay Novacek and safety James Washington in 1990.

The roster was being overhauled, and in 1990, the Cowboys began to show some signs of life.

★ ★ ★

Aikman led the Cowboys to a victory in the season opener, snapping a fourteen-game home losing streak that dated from 1988.

Three games into the season, Walsh was finally traded to the New Orleans Saints for first-, second-, and third-round picks. But most important, the

Cowboys won four straight games in November and December to move to 7–7. They had two games to go and a shot at the playoffs.

But in the next game, Troy Aikman suffered a separated shoulder and was lost for the season.

Backup quarterback Babe Laufenberg threw six interceptions in the final two games. Ironically, it was the Walsh-led Saints who made the playoffs on the final day of the regular season.

But the seeds of progress had been planted. Smith rushed for 937 yards and earned the NFL's offensive rookie of the year award. Johnson was named coach of the year.

Yet the real work was just beginning.

Johnson overhauled his offensive staff, demoting offensive coordinator David Shula and replacing him with Norv Turner. Turner became Troy's closest confidant and the man who would present him at the Pro Football Hall of Fame.

It was a move that Troy believes jump-started his career and began repairing his relationship with Johnson.

Turner installed a timing-based passing scheme

that seemed perfect for Troy and Irvin. This was complemented by a run-oriented attack that fit Smith, creating the groundwork for the team to flourish.

However, 1991 got off to a rocky start.

The Cowboys were 1–2 after the first three games. One was a shutout loss to the Philadelphia Eagles, in which Troy was sacked a whopping eleven times. It was just another example of things never seeming to go as smoothly as anticipated for the can't-miss-kid from Henryetta.

The Cowboys finally got on track, winning their next four games. But then they lost three out of four to sit at 6–5 with five games to go in the season.

Right before halftime of the next game, against the undefeated Washington Redskins, Troy hurt his knee. He began to get the nickname "Acheman" for his frequent injuries.

Steve Beuerlein, who in the offseason had replaced Laufenberg as the primary backup quarterback, came in for Aikman in the second half, and the Cowboys held on for the victory. Then Beuerlein led the Cowboys to victories in the final four games to finish the season on a five-game winning streak with an 11–5 record.

From 1–15 in 1989 to 11–5 in 1991 and their first trip to the playoffs in six years.

Emmitt Smith led the NFL in rushing with 1,563 yards, and Michael Irvin led the NFL in receiving yards. It was the first time in franchise history that the Cowboys had a player lead the league in either category, let alone both in the same season.

The city of Dallas was going crazy over the return of the Cowboys, but everything was not well.

★ ★ ★

It turned out that Troy had sprained his knee in that game against the Redskins. He sat out the final five games of the regular season as a precaution. He felt he could have returned for the season finale, but Beuerlein was playing well, and there was no need to chance it.

Johnson promised that he was saving him for the playoffs.

But when it came time for the Cowboys to face

the Chicago Bears in the playoffs, Johnson reneged on that promise. He chose Beuerlein to start the game because he had the proverbial hot hand after leading the Cowboys to five straight wins to end the season.

Now the person who was hot was Troy. It was another example of Johnson's misleading him.

"Jim and I . . . didn't really start talking till my fourth year," Troy said. "There was a stretch there where we didn't talk at all. It continued into my third year, when I got hurt."

Troy said he would have been upset at not starting the playoffs no matter what. But the way it was handled really irked him, because Johnson was dishonest about his plans.

Beuerlein started the playoff opener against the Chicago Bears, and the Cowboys won, 17–13. So he started again the next week against the Detroit Lions in what was the first playoff game in Detroit since 1957.

Detroit jumped out to a 14–3 lead, and then Troy was put in the game in hopes of mounting a comeback. But a rusty quarterback who hadn't played in seven weeks wasn't the answer. He threw an interception and fumbled two snaps in a 38–6 defeat.

Troy was so frustrated, he told local newspaper columnist Randy Galloway that he planned to ask for a trade.

"After that game, in the locker room, I just happened to run into Troy," Galloway said in the documentary *A Football Life* on the NFL Network. "And he went, 'I'm gone. I'm asking for a trade. This is not going to work.' And I didn't know if he was really serious or not. So I went, 'Well, I'm going to write that for tomorrow.'

"And Aikman went, 'Hold off. I'll call you Monday.' Sure enough, on Monday he calls and he went, 'Jimmy called me into the office a couple of hours ago. Jimmy said, "This is your team. You are my guy. No more fooling around."' And that meant more to Aikman than anything. That officially started the dynasty."

CHAPTER 6

JOHNSON PUT ACTION BEHIND his words. Even Troy recalled that the fourth season brought about a huge change in their relationship, both on and off the field.

Certainly, he was committed to Troy as a player and as a person. Johnson even installed a giant aquarium full of fish at Troy's house.

But for things to click for the Cowboys as a team on the field, he knew he needed to add some stars and playmakers on defense to go with the Triplets—Troy, Emmitt Smith, and Michael Irvin—on offense.

★ THE TRIPLETS ★

The name is so plain and simple that it belies the tour de force it represented.

They could have been called the Super Friends. Or the Three Musketeers. Or Three's Company. Or maybe even the Great Trifecta. Any of those nicknames would have fit neatly within the superhero genre of today. But Barry Switzer, who controversially replaced Jimmy Johnson in 1994, first called them the Triplets, and it stuck.

The nickname was perfect in its simplicity and symbolism, because together, quarterback Troy Aikman, receiver Michael Irvin, and running back Emmitt Smith birthed a dynasty.

"These guys revived the Cowboys in the 1990s," said Hall of Famer Roger Staubach, who was the face of the Cowboys' legendary title teams in the 1970s.

They were all great individually, coming to the Dallas Cowboys as first-round draft picks in successive years after All-American college careers. Once together as the centerpieces of the Jones and Johnson rebuilding project, they led the revival of America's team to the top of the NFL and combined for 63,201 yards and 414 touchdowns during their Hall of Fame careers.

Over the ten seasons all three were on the roster, 1990–99, the Cowboys were 101–59, a .631 winning percentage, with six division titles and eight playoff appearances.

All three were inducted into the team's hallowed Ring of Honor together in 2005 and were elected to the Pro Football Hall of Fame—Aikman in 2006, Irvin in 2007, and Smith in 2010.

And well deserved.

Irvin retired after the 1999 season, owning outright or tied for twenty Cowboys receiving records, including nearly every major career and single-season standard—career receptions (750), yardage (11,904), and hundred-yard receiving games (forty-seven). He finished his career tenth in NFL history in receptions and ninth in yardage.

His eleven hundred-yard receiving games during the 1995 season is still the NFL standard, as is the seven consecutive hundred-yard games he produced that same year. Irvin's forty-seven career hundred-yard receiving games still stands as the third most in NFL history.

Irvin was named to the Pro Bowl five times.

Smith's fifteen-year career featured four NFL rushing titles, three Super Bowl titles, and a league (1993) and Super Bowl (XXVIII) MVP award. He was selected to the Pro Bowl eight times, the second most among NFL running backs.

Smith is still the league's all-time leading rusher with 18,355 yards. He is the only player in NFL history to rush for more than 18,000 yards. Smith is also the NFL's career rushing touchdowns leader with 164, and he stands second in league annals in total touchdowns with 175.

Fittingly, their careers started together. They

are forever connected. And they are forever enshrined together.

"I can't write my life story without Emmitt and Troy," Irvin said. "They can't write their life stories without me. We're tied together forever. It's three individuals that came together as one. That's what makes it so great."

On paper and on the field, it was about passing to score and running to win. Irvin and Aikman would hook up for big plays early, with Smith grinding out the game in the fourth quarter.

Was it the passing that set up the running or the run that set up the pass?

It was about more than numbers and individual success. It was about relationships and a sacrifice for the greater good of the team that led to their success, according to Jason Garrett, the Cowboys coach and former teammate of the Triplets in the 1990s.

Garrett said coach Jimmy Johnson emphasized the importance of team. And the Triplets certainly bought into it. The approach they took every day set the standard for everybody else on the team.

"They were great players," Garrett said. "They all did an amazing job putting the team first. It wasn't ever about them. It was about winning. They pulled for each other. They complemented each other. They fought for each other. They all kept the standard high for themselves and everybody else."

Garrett emphasized the trio's unselfish play and commitment to their teammates. "It wasn't how many yards Troy threw for and how many yards Emmitt Smith had. Emmitt Smith wanted the ball because he wanted to help us win. Troy wanted the ball because he wanted to help us win. And they knew all that."

Smith, the most accomplished of the three in terms of all-time records, arguably the most decorated player in Cowboys history, agreed that their success was tied together.

"People had to prepare for all three of us," Smith said. "You could take one of us lightly if you want to, but the other two are going to hurt you pretty bad. A lot of the things I've done on the football field could not have been done without the throwing arm of Troy Aikman and the receiving arms and legs of Michael Irvin."

A picture of the famed Triplets is one of the few photos that Aikman has of his career in his house.

"That picture really symbolizes the relationship the three of us had . . . what that feeling was like, what it all meant," Troy said. "I feel wholeheartedly that our success was linked together in so many different ways. All three of us, in a lot of ways, pushed away our own egos and selfishness in order for the team to thrive."

It didn't start out as the Triplets, though.

Smith and Irvin are both from Florida and initially nicknamed themselves Double Trouble.

Irvin was always the more flamboyant one. Smith was more business-minded. But they shared familiarity and didn't know if Aikman was on board.

"Emmitt and I had put out a marketing poster of the two of us," Irvin said. "Maybe we didn't think Troy wanted to get involved. We were taking pictures on the hood of the car. We just came into something, 22 and 88. And then the thing became the Triplets. We used to talk about 'by land or by air.' My air needed Troy. It was good for Troy, too."

Irvin said what made them special is that the Triplets never had any issues or any kind of jealousy. They always respected one another's talents and what they meant to their own success.

Troy said it was because of how they came together.

He knew Irvin was great from their days playing against each other in college. Irvin had been on the opposite sideline with Jimmy Johnson and the Miami Hurricanes when they beat Aikman and the Oklahoma Sooners in 1985. That was the game where Troy broke his leg.

Irvin was already on the Cowboys when Troy was drafted, though he'd suffered a season-ending knee injury his second year.

Troy also knew Smith from college; UCLA played Smith's Florida team. A UCLA linebacker told him Smith was one of the toughest players he had ever competed against.

The threesome naturally gravitated toward one another because they were offensive skill players, high draft picks in successive years, and about the same age. So they were able to grow together, individually and collectively.

"We were a young team anyway, at the time," Troy said. "It was just kind of a natural deal. And I've always said, the best thing about Michael and [me] and Emmitt was that none of us [had] had success. Michael was the first pick in 1988, the team was 3–13, worst in football. I was the first pick in 1989, and we were 1–15. We were the worst team in football. We draft Emmitt with the first pick in '90, we go 7–9 and had a losing record. So none of us had had any success alone.

"And then when we had our success, all three of us were a part of that. We grew together and enjoyed our successes together. You know, it wasn't like one guy had already had a career and had success and we're going to bring in this other guy as the missing piece. I think that's why our Triplets were so special. It's beyond the numbers, beyond the Pro Bowls."

Aikman never led the league in any passing category. But he was always among the most efficient quarterbacks in the NFL.

His success was playing his best in big games and leading the Cowboys to Super Bowl titles as the head of the Triplets.

Ah, the Triplets.

"I loved when they called us that," Troy Aikman said.

★ ★ ★

The Cowboys drafted cornerback Kevin Smith and safety Darren Woodson in the first and second rounds, respectively, of the 1992 NFL Draft.

But the biggest move came when Johnson acquired defensive end Charles Haley from the San Francisco 49ers. There was never a question about Haley's talent. He was a three-time Pro Bowl player who had helped San Francisco win two Super Bowls. But he was also known for having mood swings. The 49ers were fed up with his bizarre behavior and practically gave him to the Cowboys for two future picks.

The question was, could the Cowboys find a way to control Haley?

With the ironfisted Johnson at the helm, that wasn't even a worry. The Cowboys had acquired their difference-maker.

"We couldn't spell Super Bowl until Charles joined us," owner Jerry Jones said. "He was our missing link."

Troy, who once called Haley one of the scariest dudes he had ever been around, didn't take long to be convinced.

Never mind that upon arriving in Dallas, Haley told a Cowboys beat writer for the *Fort Worth Star-Telegram* that Troy Aikman didn't measure up to San Francisco 49ers quarterback Joe Montana.

"I love the guy to death," Aikman said of Haley. "He was a consummate professional in my opinion. He wasn't always during the week, but boy on Sunday, he sure was. . . . Nobody brought it like he did on game day."

With Haley, the Cowboys featured the league's top-ranked defense for the first time since 1977—the last time they'd won the Super Bowl. It all proved to be a good omen for a Cowboys team that many considered a year away from making a Super Bowl run.

This bunch of Troy Aikman–led upstarts began the season 3–0 en route to a 13–3 finish. Aikman was the general on the field, but Johnson was the master manipulator who twisted the screws off the field.

Consider the season finale against the Chicago Bears. The Cowboys saw their 27–0 lead dwindle to 27–14 because backup running back Curvin Richards had two fumbles in the fourth quarter after replacing Emmitt Smith.

Smith was the NFL's rushing champ for a second straight season, recording a club-record 1,713 yards. Richards was a little-used backup. Still, Johnson cut Richards the next day, sending a message to the rest of the team that he was focused on winning it all now and wasn't going to tolerate mistakes.

Interestingly enough, it was that game that offered outward signs of the fraying relationship between Jimmy Johnson and Jerry Jones.

Jones liked to host dignitaries and celebrities in his suite at games, and sometimes he took them to the sidelines and the locker room after the game. This angered the football-focused Johnson.

Jones took Prince Bandar bin Sultan, a Saudi Arabian ambassador and a huge Cowboys fan, to the sidelines along with his bodyguards.

Johnson was none too pleased.

But they survived, and the Cowboys set off on their journey of making history.

They put a 34–10 whipping on the Philadelphia Eagles, who had acquired former running back Herschel Walker after he flamed out in Minnesota.

Troy was an efficient fifteen of twenty-five,

passing for two hundred yards, with two touchdowns and no interceptions, earning his first playoff victory.

The Cowboys then went on the road to face the favored San Francisco 49ers in the NFC championship game for the right to go to the Super Bowl.

The 49ers, led by future Hall of Famers Steve Young and Jerry Rice, had the league's top-ranked offense.

Again, the Cowboys had the top-ranked defense, led by Haley, in a game that was billed as the real Super Bowl.

But the Cowboys also had Aikman, who proved to play his best in the biggest games and the biggest moments.

Up 24–20 with 4:22 left in the game, Aikman threw a perfect strike to receiver Alvin Harper on a slant. Harper caught it in stride, split the defense, and ran seventy yards before being tackled. Troy finished the drive off with a six-yard touchdown pass to Kelvin Martin, securing a 30–20 victory.

Troy's numbers against the 49ers were spectacular, passing for 322 yards and two touchdowns, with no interceptions. Yet even that performance didn't provide Aikman any grace with the focused Johnson. He actually left Troy at the stadium after the game!

"A big win in the NFC championship game, going to the Super Bowl," Troy recalled with a laugh. "What I remember most, however, was ... I had to do a lot of interviews following that game. And as we walked out of the locker room finally, I started to find and locate the bus, and Jimmy had told the bus drivers, 'Close the doors; we're leaving.' They said, 'Wait a minute; Aikman's not on the bus yet.' He said, 'I don't care; we're leaving him.' I had to basically take public transit from Candlestick Park to the team charter. Now, are you kidding me?"

Johnson was ready to get to the plane and start preparing for the Super Bowl.

CHAPTER 7

AH, THE SUPER BOWL.

The journey that had started with the drafting of Troy first overall in 1989 was finally complete. Super Bowl XXVII against the Buffalo Bills was simply the icing on the cake for Troy and the Cowboys.

It was even more special because the game was played in Pasadena, California, the city where Troy had played in college. The Cowboys even practiced at UCLA.

Troy was able to bond with friends and family as well as enjoy the comfort of a familiar setting. There were no nerves heading into what proved to be a perfect Super Bowl performance.

"Yeah it was helpful for me . . . the support staff that we picked up—many of [them] were equipment guys when I was playing, so there was some familiarity for me throughout the week and [throughout] my preparation. And I think it allowed me to be a little more at ease. It certainly did on game day.

"We dressed in the home locker room where I had for UCLA as well, and I was familiar with the stadium and the surroundings and what that would be like. I think it was really helpful for me. . . . I never really slept great the night before games, but the night before my first Super Bowl, I slept very well. And was pleasantly surprised—leading up to the game and in the locker room, I was a little more at ease and calm than I typically am."

The Cowboys won, 52–17, in a game that was seemingly a blowout from the outset.

Although they'd trailed 7–0 in the first quarter, thanks to a blocked punt, they were shaken but not deterred.

"What we didn't want to happen, happened," guard Nate Newton said after the game. "We just had to settle down a little. We had to clear our heads.

One play is not going to make or break us. We had plenty more ball to play."

Did they ever—and quickly.

The Cowboys scored two touchdowns fifteen seconds apart. Troy threw a touchdown pass to tight end Jay Novacek. Then defensive end Jimmie Jones scored a touchdown on a two-yard fumble return.

The Cowboys then scored two touchdowns in three plays in an eighteen-second span. Troy tossed scores of nineteen and eighteen yards to Michael Irvin, with another Jimmie Jones fumble recovery sandwiched in between.

In total, Troy was almost a perfect fourteen of eighteen, passing for 148 yards and three touchdowns as the Cowboys built a 28–10 lead.

They simply cruised from there.

And then the party would begin.

Troy was named the game's most valuable player. The Cowboys were the youngest team in football.

And it was not lost on Troy that four years before, the Cowboys had been 1–15, and he was 0–11 as the starter of the worst team in football.

He had endured a lot since his days in tiny

Henryetta, where his biggest initial adjustment was hauling hay and feeding farm animals.

Then there was the broken leg at Oklahoma.

The transfer to UCLA.

The Steve Walsh drama.

The Steve Beuerlein controversy.

But now Aikman was on top of the world.

"This game means everything to me," he said as he held the Lombardi Trophy. "A tremendous weight has been lifted from my shoulders. No matter what happens the rest of my career, I can say I took a team to a Super Bowl and won it. There aren't too many who can say that. This is as great a feeling as I've ever had in my life."

CHAPTER 8

HOW ABOUT BACK-TO-BACK Super Bowl wins?

"These guys have a chance to go back-to-back," Charles Haley said after the game. "If we stay unselfish and guys don't hold out of camp, we and Coach Johnson can win a lot of these."

The winning of one title with such a young team only fostered talk of the Cowboys' winning multiple titles. And why not? Troy, Emmitt Smith, and Michael Irvin were in their prime. The defense remained strong, and the Cowboys still had the best and most focused coach in football in Jimmy Johnson.

But the Cowboys, who had taken four years to

climb to the top of the NFL world, would quickly learn about the cost of staying on top.

Emmitt Smith went from the first NFL rushing champion to win a Super Bowl to winning back-to-back rushing titles. Now he wanted more money. He and owner Jerry Jones were in a standoff. So he held out of training camp and missed the first two games of the season.

The Cowboys lost those first two games. The walls literally started caving in on Jones. Charles Haley was so angry after the loss to the Buffalo Bills in the second game of the season that he put a dent in the wall in the Cowboys locker room.

Jones relented and gave Smith a four-year, $13.6 million deal.

Not coincidentally, Jones rewarded Troy with an eight-year, $50 million deal later in the season, making him at that point the highest-paid player in NFL history. The twenty-seven-year-old quarterback would receive an $11 million signing bonus and salaries ranging from $1.75 million in 1994 to $7.5 million in 2000.

Upon Smith's return, the Cowboys promptly

embarked on a seven-game winning streak. The team lost just twice more that season, winning back-to-back NFC East titles and finishing the season 12–4.

Smith became the first player to win the rushing title (his third straight) after missing the first two games. He became the first—and is still the only—player in Cowboys history to be named the NFL's most valuable player.

He cemented his legacy in the division-clinching victory against the New York Giants in the season finale, rushing for 168 yards on thirty-two carries while playing with a painful separated shoulder.

But despite Smith's heroics, this was a fractured team entering the playoffs.

Another sign of a splinter between Jerry Jones and Jimmy Johnson had come during the season. Johnson had expressed interest in becoming the coach and general manager of a new franchise in Jacksonville. But Johnson was still under contract, so if a team wanted him, they would have to compensate the Cowboys. Jones said it would cost two first-round picks to get Johnson away from Dallas.

But history soon let everyone know that it would cost considerably less.

★ ★ ★

Troy saved the Cowboys in the playoff opener against the Green Bay Packers. He passed for 302 yards and three touchdowns to outduel future Hall of Famer Brett Favre in a 27–17 victory.

It set up a rematch with the San Francisco 49ers in the NFC championship game.

Johnson put even more pressure on the Cowboys when he called a local radio show and told newspaper columnist Randy Galloway that the Cowboys would win the game. "And you can put it in three-inch headlines: We will win the ball game!"

Sure enough, the Cowboys had a twenty-one-point lead at halftime, well on their way to a 38–21 victory.

But Troy has no memory of any of it.

He threw two early touchdowns on a near-perfect fourteen-of-eighteen passing. Then early in the third quarter, he took a knee to the head. He was knocked out of the game with a concussion.

Backup quarterback Bernie Kosar finished the game that took the Cowboys to their seventh Super Bowl.

Troy was so out of it that he said the upcoming Super Bowl was going to be played in his hometown of Henryetta, Oklahoma.

Troy's agent, Leigh Steinberg, gave an even more chilling recollection of the situation during a PBS *Frontline* documentary on concussions called *League of Denial.*

Steinberg visited Troy in a darkened hospital room because his concussed eyes were sensitive to the light.

"He looked at me, and he said, 'Leigh, where am I?' And I said, 'Well, you're in the hospital,'" Steinberg said. "And he said, 'Well, why am I here?' And I said, 'Because you suffered a concussion today.' And he said, 'Well, who did we play?' And I said, 'The Forty-Niners.' And he said, 'Did we win?' 'Yes, you won.' 'Did I play well?' 'Yes, you played well.' 'And so what's that mean?' 'It means you're going to the Super Bowl.'"

Five minutes later, Aikman turned to Steinberg and said, "What am I doing here?"

They repeated the initial conversation all over again.

Making the situation even more serious was that the Super Bowl rematch against the Buffalo Bills was to be played the following week.

There would not be two weeks between games. It was just one week between games. Troy didn't have a lot of time to get over the concussion.

Remember, this is Kenneth Aikman's son. He was raised to be tough.

Troy still has no recollection of the 1993 NFC championship game. But it has not affected him now, and he didn't worry about it then.

"They say once you have one [a concussion], the chances of it occurring again are greater. But I don't worry about it.... It's part of playing the game," Troy said to reporters two days after the game as he prepared for the Super Bowl.

Troy was solid, but he passed for just 207 yards and didn't throw a touchdown pass. Still, the Cowboys beat the Buffalo Bills, 30–13, to win a second straight title.

The defense and running back Emmitt Smith brought this one home.

Trailing 13-6 at halftime, the Cowboys got a spark from safety James Washington. Three plays into the third quarter, he returned a fumble forty-six yards for a touchdown to tie the game. Washington was a good bet to win most valuable player because he also had a forced fumble and an interception in the game.

But that honor went to Smith, who rushed for 132 yards and two touchdowns to cap a season in which he added a Super Bowl MVP award to his league MVP honor.

"Our mission is completed," Smith said. "We came into this season with the idea of doing this. It's been a super year for me as well as my teammates. Being MVP of the league and this game, you can't ask for anything more."

Suddenly, this was no longer just the start of something special. This had the making of something historic.

"It's too early to call us the Team of the Nineties," Troy said after the game. "But I guess this says last year was not a fluke. It puts us with some great teams. What exactly that means to all of us, I'm not sure.

"Last year's Super Bowl was one of disbelief, a bunch of young, bright-eyed guys caught up in it all. This is one of satisfaction because the expectations were so much higher."

Back-to-back champs.

"I'm not much of a historian," said coach Jimmy Johnson. "I just know we've won two Super Bowls in a row."

CHAPTER 9

NOW THE COWBOYS STARTED thinking about doing something unprecedented.

How about a three-peat?

The notion wasn't lost on giddy and Super Bowl-greedy owner Jerry Jones.

"We have a great opportunity to do something that has never been done, and that's to win three straight Super Bowls," Jones said. "I know that Jimmy enjoys challenges, and I know that he will be here."

And why not?

Who would pass up a chance to make a run at a third straight Super Bowl title?

That's certainly what Troy thought as well.

His problems with Johnson earlier in his career have been well documented.

But at this point, they were the best of friends.

Johnson had set up an aquarium in Troy's house. Sometimes he would come over and visit the fish.

"He would call me up on a Tuesday, on the day off, and say, 'Hey, what are you doing?'" Troy said. "I said, 'I'm just at home.' He said, 'Hey, I got Rhonda. We're going to come over and just check out your fish.' I said, 'Okay.' He'd come over . . . and sit. The aquarium was in my bedroom, so he'd come into my bedroom, have a chair, just relax, and . . . he and his wife, Rhonda, [would] sit there and talk fish and all that."

It was a relationship that Troy cherished. He had never had that before with a head coach.

Part of him believed that Jimmy Johnson would stay because of him and their relationship.

Times were finally really good for Troy.

★ ★ ★

But then something happened after the NFL owners meeting. Johnson was with some friends, including former Cowboys staffers Dave Wannstedt and Norv Turner, who had left to take jobs with other teams. Jones walked up and offered to toast the coaches and their success. He became upset that he hadn't been invited to join them.

Jones later declared to reporters that he might fire Johnson, defiantly saying that "five hundred coaches could have won the Super Bowl with the Cowboys."

And just like that, it was over.

Two months after winning back-to-back Super Bowls, Johnson and Jones were no more.

It was March 29 when Jones and Johnson held a news conference to announce their divorce. Johnson was given a $2 million parting gift.

And Jones was now firmly in charge of everything.

The breakup was shocking.

Back-to-back Super Bowl champs. A chance to win a third straight title with the most talented roster in the NFL, led by future Hall of Famers Troy, Emmitt, and Michael in the prime of their careers. Who breaks that up?

"You know, it was a really special deal, but it

In 1989, Troy Aikman was drafted first overall by the Dallas Cowboys.

In 1994, all players wore the "NFL 75" logo to mark the league's anniversary.

Troy Aikman watches intently from the sideline.

Aikman celebrates after winning his second
Super Bowl in a row.

Coach Jimmy Johnson and Troy Aikman hug following the Cowboys' Super Bowl XXVIII win.

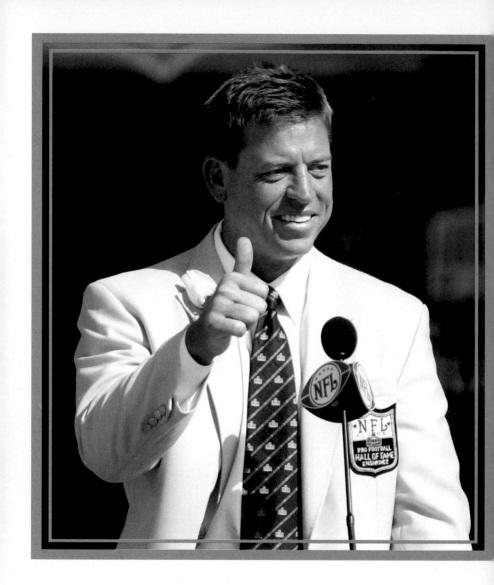

Aikman gives a thumbs-up to the crowd
after being enshrined in the Pro Football
Hall of Fame in 2006.

Aikman unveils his Hall of Fame bust, one of the three icons—Bronze Bust, Gold Jacket, and Ring of Excellence.

Aikman is honored as a Hometown Hall of Famer in Henryetta, Oklahoma.

happened too soon for all of us," Troy said. "No one appreciated it."

What disappointed Troy the most was the hypocrisy of it all.

He recalled Jimmy's standing up in front of the team and saying that if they do what they are supposed to do, there would be enough success and credit to go around for everybody.

He always preached that everything was about the team and that individual players shouldn't worry if they didn't get named to the Pro Bowl as some others did.

"But the two people that were preaching it the most weren't doing it," Troy said. "Jerry wanted all the attention; Jimmy wanted all the attention; and they both said, 'Hey, it's about me.' So that's the only part of that that really upsets me."

The Cowboys had something special.

But it could have been historic.

★ ★ ★

Interestingly enough, if the Jones-Johnson breakup had not taken place a full fifty-eight days after the

Super Bowl but had happened in the immediate aftermath of the game, the keys to the championship car might have been passed down to offensive coordinator Norv Turner, Troy's closest confidant.

Turner was now in Washington as the new coach of the Redskins.

So Jones tapped into another former Arkansas connection: former Oklahoma coach Barry Switzer, who was on the staff at Arkansas when Jerry and Jimmy helped the team win a national title.

Yes, the same Switzer whom Troy played for his first two years in college, before transferring to UCLA.

Switzer was, indeed, a championship coach on the college level. But he had been out of coaching since being forced to resign at Oklahoma in 1988 because of a number of scandals in his football program. He knew nothing of the ways of the NFL, but he was Jones's handpicked man to replace Johnson.

It wasn't lost on anyone that Johnson and Switzer had been adversaries in college, first when Johnson was at Oklahoma State and then when Johnson was at Miami.

They also had two different coaching styles. Johnson was hard-nosed, and Switzer was laid-back.

No one knew the difference more than Troy.

But for what it's worth, Troy was not against the hire initially. He didn't want Johnson gone. But he wasn't necessarily against the hiring of Switzer if he was going to be the committed coach that he had been at Oklahoma.

"Jerry asked me, he said, 'Hey, this thing with Jimmy, it's going to go down, and if it does, we're going to have to move quick. I just want to know what you think about that.' I said, 'I don't want to talk about that. I want . . . Jimmy to stay.' I said, 'Jerry, I'm not comfortable talking about the job that's not open.'"

But Jones persisted, prompting Troy to say, "If Jimmy is no longer the head coach, I think Switzer would be great."

In fact, Troy was the one who calmed his teammates down at the beginning and told them to give Switzer a chance.

Because, at the outset, it was utter chaos in the Cowboys locker room.

Michael Irvin, who had played for Johnson in college at Miami, was going berserk, throwing trash cans.

"He was upset," Troy said. "He's throwing trash cans, and I'm the one going around the locker room. . . . [I] met up with Michael, and with all these guys, and said, 'Hey, you're going to love Barry.'"

Troy felt that way because he thought Switzer was going to be 100 percent committed. And he said the transition was hard at first. It turned out that Switzer liked to party as much as the players.

"It became really tough when I realized that it was a coach who really had very little interest in coaching," Troy said.

And besides losing Johnson and adding Switzer, the Cowboys continued to lose talent in free agency. Core members of the two-time Super Bowl champions were leaving, with no equivalent replacements.

The problem was intensified by a tight salary cap and the loss of Johnson's eye for talent.

But the Triplets were still there, so no one was feeling sorry for the back-to-back champs.

When the Cowboys reached mid-season with an

8-1 record, it appeared to be business as usual. Troy then threw three interceptions in a 21–14 loss to the 49ers.

But the Cowboys won the next game and were 9-2 when they faced the Green Bay Packers on Thanksgiving. They had to play without Troy, who had injured his knee, and without backup Rodney Peete.

The Cowboys turned to third-stringer Jason Garrett in pulling off a miracle 42–31 victory against the Packers. It's the same Garrett who would one day become the team's eighth head coach.

The Cowboys lost two of the final four games but finished 12–4 to win the NFC East for the third straight season.

With Troy healthy again, they blasted the Packers in the first playoff game by a score of 35–9.

Up next was the third straight showdown against the 49ers in the NFC championship game for the right to go to the Super Bowl.

This time they would face the 49ers without Jimmy Johnson.

This time Emmitt Smith would enter the game

less than 100 percent because of a hamstring injury at the end of the season.

This time the 49ers had superstar free-agent cornerback Deion Sanders on their side.

And this time the Cowboys self-destructed right from the start.

The Cowboys trailed, 21–0, five minutes into the game. Troy threw an interception that Eric Davis returned forty-four yards for a touchdown. Irvin fumbled and receiver Kevin Williams fumbled a kickoff that the 49ers turned into touchdowns.

"Giving San Francisco a twenty-one-point lead is like spotting Carl Lewis twenty yards in the hundred-yard dash," Smith said.

Fittingly, Lewis, an Olympic sprint champion, was known for his closing kick. The Cowboys did their best Lewis impression to almost nip the 49ers at the finish line.

The Cowboys refused to give up. They made it 24–14 late in the first half. Troy threw a forty-four-yard touchdown pass to Irvin, and Smith had a four-yard run. The Cowboys got the ball back right before halftime, but rather than sit on the ball, they tried to score. But three straight incomplete passes gave the ball back to the 49ers with time on the clock. Future Hall of Fame quarterback Steve Young tossed a twenty-eight-yard touchdown pass to future Hall of Fame receiver Jerry Rice, who beat cornerback Larry Brown on man-to-man coverage, making the score 31–14 at halftime.

Barry Switzer complained about the soggy field conditions and bias by the officials against the Cowboys. Looking back, he said that was the biggest difference in the game that denied them the opportunity to become the first team in history to win three straight Super Bowl titles.

It continues to bother him to this day. He said he always thinks about it because it denied the Cowboys an opportunity to do something historic.

"We didn't give ourselves a chance. We were down...21–0 [in] five minutes," Switzer recalled. "Like I told 'em, thank God we got fifty-five minutes to get back in this.... We got back within [ten] in the first half, and I made a mistake. I let [offensive coordinator] Ernie Zampese talk me into going. I said, 'Ernie, run the ball three times and...if we have to punt it away, if we don't move the chains, they'll have no time left offensively.' He said, 'No . . . we can get a field goal. We've got it going now. We can score.' I let him talk me into it. We throw three incomplete passes. We punt the ball away. They get it with fifty-six seconds left. They hit Jerry Rice over Larry Brown in the end zone at halftime. . . . You think I didn't dog-cuss myself all the way to the locker room? That bothers the hell out of me. I remember every play of it."

But this was a game Troy and his teammates from those title teams of the 1990s are most proud of.

It proved they were more than just glitz and glamour. They were more than just a collection of high draft picks.

They truly had the hearts of champions.

The Cowboys died hard that day in San Francisco. There was definitely no quit in a team that had Troy as its leader.

A touchdown pass to Irvin and a score on the ground by Smith had the Cowboys down just ten, 38–28, early in the fourth quarter.

The Cowboys appeared to be driving again when

Deion Sanders, who had been covering Alvin Harper most of the day, finally locked up with Irvin and shoved him to the ground on a pass close to the end zone.

It was clearly pass interference.

An irate Switzer was penalized for bumping an official in his disgust.

But instead of a first and goal with an opportunity to trim the 49ers' lead to three, the Cowboys were marched back fifteen yards and eventually turned the ball over on downs. That ended the comeback.

Switzer went after the officials and the conditions. The Cowboys missed a twenty-seven-yard field goal in the muddy quagmire.

"That's a disgrace to play championship football on a field like that," Switzer said. "Why didn't the league do something about that?"

Owner Jerry Jones immediately went on to defend his decision to fire Johnson and hire Switzer.

"There is nothing we need to change to beat the Forty-Niners. This team has proved it can handle as many distractions as you want to heap upon it," Jones said. "I chose to make that decision, and I'm not going to second-guess it."

The players took the loss hard.

A despondent Charles Haley announced his retirement in the postgame locker room. Later, he rescinded it.

But the Cowboys walked away with their heads held high because of the way they played and performed in the face of adversity, not just in the championship game but all season after Johnson's departure.

"When I'm sixty and I tell my grandchildren about this team," Irvin said, "I will tell them with pride about a team that just kept bouncing back. But let me tell you this, losing's rough."

It was rough on Troy as well.

His uniform was as muddy afterward as it had ever been. But he walked away with more pride in his team and himself after a loss than he ever had in his career.

Troy completed thirty of fifty-three passes for 380 yards, with two touchdowns and three interceptions on the day, but it was his leadership and fight that stood out most to his teammates.

"I think that game, to me, is the game I'm most proud of," Troy said.

At that point, most of America knew the Cowboys as champions. They had forgotten the 1–15 season. All they knew were the rock-star Cowboys who dominated the national scene because of their play on the field and the headlines they made off it.

"We were winning, and all of a sudden we were winning big," Troy said. "They don't remember that Michael was 3–13, I was 1–15. So what America saw of us was a team who was just winning. And . . . so for the first time, the nation, the country, got to see us down, you know. We were down. And the way that we came back and continued to fight, I think that we showed the country why we had been champions, why we had been back-to-back champions, and what we were made of. I never felt real good coming out of a game after a loss. But I did after that one. I was disappointed, but I was really proud of the way we played and fought. I wish we'd played our best football."

CHAPTER 10

NOW THAT THE COWBOYS had been knocked off their lofty pedestal, the question was whether they could return to the top.

They firmly believed that if they had played their best football, they would have beaten the 49ers and gone on to capture their third straight Super Bowl title.

They were forced to forge ahead in 1995 after a continued drain in their talent in free agency.

It was something they understood immediately after the NFC championship game.

"It's going to be hard to build a dynasty," receiver Alvin Harper said. "The Cowboys are going to lose a lot of key players, including myself. The money is just not going to be there.

"For me, it just hurts real bad, because I didn't want to go out a loser. I wanted to go to the Super Bowl, win, and then go out and test the free-agent market."

Harper left. So did Kenny Gant, Jim Jeffcoat, Mark Stepnoski, and James Washington. This was after losing the likes of Ken Norton, Tony Casillas, Jimmie Jones, Kevin Gogan, and John Gesek the year before.

They weren't the Triplets, but they were all key contributors on the back-to-back title teams and part of the reason the Cowboys were considered to have the most talent in the league.

But that was gone—as was the architect of it all, Jimmy Johnson.

It didn't help that Switzer's lax ways and inattention to detail started to permeate the organization.

"It got ugly when Barry came," former Cowboys running backs coach Joe Brodsky said. "There was a lot going on behind the scenes."

The Cowboys still had Troy, Emmitt, and Michael, so they remained one of the top teams in the league.

The 1995 season got off to a great start with a 35–0 victory against the New York Giants. But cornerback Kevin Smith was lost for the season in the game with a torn Achilles tendon.

And now Jerry Jones, who was already in the market to land superstar cornerback Deion Sanders—the same Sanders who'd helped the 49ers beat the Cowboys the year before—was in desperation mode.

Jones was a gambler by nature and a rebel. He had been bucking the NFL since he'd bought the Cowboys in 1989.

And that same week of the opener against the Giants, he rocked the league again with a seven-year contract with Nike and Texas Stadium that wouldn't be part of the NFL's revenue-sharing deal.

So the Cowboys were suddenly flush with money to get the deal done with Sanders.

But the situation caused an uncomfortable moment with Jones and his son Stephen Jones, who was the team's salary-cap expert. And considering the recent departures in free agency, the money wasn't looking all that good.

The Cowboys subsequently signed Sanders to a five-year, $35 million contract to play cornerback, some offense, and return kicks for the Dallas Cowboys that season.

It made him the second-highest-paid Cowboy behind Troy's $50 million deal. According to Jones, Troy agreed to restructure his contract so the Cowboys could get Sanders under the salary cap that season.

Still, Sanders's bonus of $12.9 million was virtually equal to Emmitt Smith's entire contract.

"I know the dollar situation isn't a problem on this team," Irvin said at the time. "I hope nobody tries to make it a problem. . . . I've never seen him play wide receiver, but maybe he will take some of those slant passes over the middle. I could use a good decoy, too. You can never have too many of them."

Jones believed that adding Sanders, the league's reigning defensive player of the year, swung the balance of power back to the Cowboys and made them Super Bowl favorites again.

It didn't matter that Sanders wouldn't join until after the baseball season—he played outfield for the San Francisco Giants at the time.

"I know people said I paid too much, but anytime in my life I have paid too much for anything, it has been for quality," Jones said.

The Cowboys waited eight games for Sanders to make his debut. They were 6–1 at the time. They beat the Atlanta Falcons for his first game, but tumult would soon hit. Defensive tackle Leon Lett and cornerback Clayton Holmes were suspended for four games for violating the substance-abuse policy.

The Cowboys soon improved to 8–1 on the season, but they weren't playing well—and certainly not up to Troy's standards. Their next game was against the 49ers—a team that came into the game with a 5–4 record. After falling behind 24–0, Dallas lost, 38–20.

But after two solid victories and a loss to the Washington Redskins would come the signature game of Switzer's tenure.

★ ★ ★

On a bitterly cold day on the road against the Phila-delphia Eagles, Dallas blew a fourteen-point lead. Now tied, with just over two minutes left in the game, the Cowboys faced fourth and inches from their own 29-yard line.

Switzer decided to go for it in an attempt to give the struggling offense a boost.

He called Load Left, one of the team's signature plays. Emmitt Smith went left behind guard Nate Newton and tackle Mark Tuinei.

The Eagles knew what was coming and stopped Smith for no gain.

"We know it's coming; they know it's coming," Newton said. "The whole world knows it's com-ing."

The Cowboys seemingly got a miracle reprieve when it was ruled that the two-minute warning hit before the ball was snapped, stopping the clock for a timeout.

So this was the perfect opportunity for Switzer to change his mind and punt the ball away.

But Switzer not only decided to go for it again but also called the same play again: Load Left.

The Eagles were all over it. They took over the ball and kicked the game-winning field goal.

"I'm going, 'Don't do this.' Not the same play," remembered Daryl Johnston in Norm Hitzges's 2007 book *Greatest Team Ever*. "They had seven guys at the point of attack, and we're doing the same thing?

"You're just hoping Troy is gonna say, 'This isn't right.' Call a timeout. Explain your point. Hey, we'll do this, but give us a different play."

It was arrogance. It was confidence. It was dumb.

Switzer was roundly criticized for the call.

He was nicknamed Bozo the coach, and the decision was called the sequel to *Dumb and Dumber*.

To Cowboys fans, it was all seemingly a realization of the worst nightmares they'd had when Switzer replaced Johnson as coach.

Poor decision making. An inattention to detail.

The necessary elements were all lacking.

On top of everything else, Troy and Switzer were not on speaking terms. Switzer's poor discipline and lack of commitment to excellence had never sat well with Aikman, and the situation had now reached a boiling point.

Asked after the game if he would think about replacing Switzer if the Cowboys failed to reach the Super Bowl, especially considering what he had paid to sign Sanders, Jones remained steadfast.

"There won't be any coaching changes," Jones said. "He'll be back next year. Definitely."

Instead of making the Cowboys fall apart, the game seemed to bring them together. It proved to be their rallying cry, fostered in the locker room after the Eagles game with a heartfelt speech from Switzer.

"I wanted them to know I believed in them because I made that call," Switzer said. "And I didn't give up on them—that's why I made it again. I believed in them, and I wanted them to believe in me. I didn't turn on them, and I didn't want them to turn on me. . . . 'Coaches make dumb mistakes, along with players who make dumb mistakes, but we win or lose together,' I told them. Don't let people outside this room, the media, affect where we are, because we're still going to arrive where we want to arrive."

They won their final two games to finish 12–4.

The Cowboys came back to beat the Giants by one point. They got a gift in the season finale, when the 49ers lost, allowing them to clinch home-field advantage with a win against the Arizona Cardinals on Christmas night on *Monday Night Football*.

It was the game featured in the movie *Jerry Maguire*, and Troy made a cameo appearance.

"We had a stretch there where we were not good," Troy said. "We beat the Giants in Texas Stadium. . . . Kevin Williams laid out an unbelievable catch of the ball. It got a first down; we win the game. I don't know what might have happened had we not won that game, but it wasn't going to be good. We were really struggling offensively, big-time. And then the last game of the season, we were playing on Christmas night at Arizona. And the Forty-Niners, they had home-field advantage.

"And then they lose to Atlanta. And we're on the plane, flying to Arizona, and . . . they announce that San Francisco had lost, and what that meant was if we won on Christmas night, we were going to get home-field advantage."

As Troy said, the Cowboys struggled on offense late in the season. But they came out and lit up the Cardinals in a 37–13 victory.

"It propelled us all the way to the Super Bowl,"

Troy said. "So that '95 team ... people that didn't really know what all was going on behind the scenes, they kind of laugh, but it might have been the greatest team in sports. I mean that team was complete [chaos]. Just kind of pulled it together at the right time."

It did come together again for the Cowboys in 1995. The Green Bay Packers, led by rising superstar quarterback Brett Favre, upset the 49ers in the divisional playoffs.

The Cowboys got revenge on the Eagles and Load Left with a 30–11 victory. Sanders delivered the goods with an interception and a touchdown on a reverse.

The only thing that stood between the Cowboys and their third trip to the Super Bowl in four years— and possibly their third title in four years—was the Green Bay Packers in the NFC championship game.

Troy outdueled Favre, reigning league MVP, in what he calls the finest playoff game of his career.

Fittingly, it was because it was a complete team win. Troy passed for 255 yards and two touchdowns to Irvin. Smith rushed thirty-five times for 150 yards.

And the Cowboys rallied from a 27–24 deficit

with two touchdowns in the fourth quarter to seal the 38–27 victory and the trip to Super Bowl XXX against the Pittsburgh Steelers in Tempe, Arizona.

"This football team has been in this situation before," Aikman said. "We get the ball late in the fourth quarter and you have to take time off the clock to put them away, and we were able to do that.

"I know Barry thought we had to score thirty points to win the football game, and I really thought that was unrealistic in any game. But that's how it turned out. I expected a tough ball game. I knew they would put some points up."

Switzer certainly ate it up, and Irvin gave him his due after the game.

"We're going to the Super Bowl," Irvin said. "We let someone else borrow our house last year. We're going home. That's where we belong. There is nobody who deserves this more than Barry Switzer."

Troy felt so good that he gave Switzer the game ball after the game.

"Look, I don't want you guys to make a big deal out of me giving him the football," Troy said. "There is still something left for this football team to achieve. I know that I'm not content, and I don't think this team is."

Troy was talking about winning the Super Bowl amid the Switzer-hyped hysteria of getting there.

But the pain of that relationship would soon return.

It was revealed during media interviews Super Bowl week that one of Switzer's former assistants accused Troy of being overly critical of his black teammates.

Michael Irvin, who is black, and several other players came out in support of Troy, but the damage was done.

"I stood up. I put a stop to that," Irvin said. "Man, please. Get out of here with that stuff. I was like, stop that, man. We are winning like we are winning, and so much mess gets started. We never had any issues."

There was still another layer to the turbulent Super Bowl week. The debauchery and lack of discipline of the Cowboys under Switzer was also revealed to the world.

Several players had limousines driven to Arizona from Dallas to party in. Not to be outdone, Switzer hosted parties nightly in his hotel suite, running up a tab of $100,000. Owner Jerry Jones also rented a party bus for the week.

Practice during the week was an afterthought. Players came in limos after a night of partying.

The Cowboys were heavy favorites. So they didn't take the Steelers seriously.

They didn't play well, but they won 27–17. Cornerback Larry Brown earned Super Bowl MVP honors because of two gift-wrapped interceptions.

Switzer felt vindicated.

"We did it our way, baby! We did it!" he yelled after the game.

Jerry Jones felt satisfied to finally win one without Jimmy Johnson.

And the Cowboys cemented themselves as the team of the 1990s with their third Super Bowl title. In fact, Troy's Cowboys were the first team in NFL history to win three Super Bowls in four years. They were already a bona fide dynasty.

Irvin called this one the sweetest of them all because of the controversy during the season.

"You can put the other two together, and this

one outweighs them," Irvin said. "That's because of what we went through, because of the times people counted us out. . . . Bottom line, we got it done."

It was a miracle they got it done, according to Troy.

It's why he said they had to be one of the greatest teams ever. They had to overcome so much turmoil.

"We won the Super Bowl, which is pretty . . . incredible," Troy said. "Barry and I weren't speaking. We didn't speak at all the second half of the season. We didn't speak the week of the Super Bowl. The elevator opened up one night and he's getting off, I'm getting on. We just walked right past each other."

CHAPTER 11

AIKMAN HOPED THE DRAMA would end after the Super Bowl. It was his understanding that Switzer would be replaced after the game, win or lose.

He said Jerry Jones implied that Switzer would not be back.

Of course, days after the game, Jones called Troy to his house and explained to him why Switzer would stay on as coach for two more seasons.

As fast and steep as the Cowboys' climb to the top was, the decline would prove to be just as precipitous.

It was not just about Switzer. A lack of discipline off the field ran amok throughout the team. It started to take its toll on the Cowboys.

Troy said so much stuff was going on that there were cameras in the dorm room at training camp.

"It had gotten to where there was just no organizational patrol, you know," Troy said. "So we kind of lost our way. From a discipline standpoint, things had gotten a little looser and a little more lax, and nobody was . . . holding people accountable. And so we continued to get worse and worse and worse. So it's frustrating."

It was frustrating because of the work ethic and level of discipline Troy had grown up with. He had found a kindred spirit in Jimmy Johnson in terms of his attention to detail.

But with Johnson gone, Troy came across as the bad cop all the time. He was the only one trying to hold people accountable.

Ironically, it was in 1995 that Troy coauthored his first book for children, *Things Change*. He encouraged kids to treat setbacks and changes not as frustrating times to get through but as chances to grow in unexpected ways.

He talked about his childhood and the move from California to rural Oklahoma, how his interest in football developed, his successes and failures in high school and college sports, and his professional career, including his three trips to the Super Bowl.

It was a book for kids, but it was something Troy could lean on himself.

The true turning point of the downslide for the Cowboys came two months after the Super Bowl, when Michael Irvin was arrested on drug possession charges.

The subsequent trial made national headlines.

Troy was the only teammate who showed up in court to support Irvin.

Irvin was his favorite receiver. The two long had a close personal relationship.

It's also what leaders do. He didn't condone Irvin's action, but he was there to support his teammate.

Irvin asked his family not to come to the courtroom and sit through those proceedings. But the sight of Troy coming in and sitting there was special to him, particularly considering their different upbringings, backgrounds, life experiences, and personalities.

Troy was a California kid who had grown up on a farm in tiny Henryetta, Oklahoma. Irvin had grown up among seventeen brothers and sisters in Miami.

They came from completely different worlds.

"That showed his maturity," Irvin said. "That meant a lot for him showing up. I knew he wanted to do it.

"I was cool with him not doing it. But he did it anyway. It was something. I can imagine some of the things that I grew up around, Troy wouldn't even understand. It was big. It was incredible. I was thinking about the young Michael. And the young Troy walking in there. Wow. That's something."

Irvin ended up pleading no contest and was suspended five games by the NFL.

★ ★ ★

The Cowboys went 2–3 at the start of the 1996 season without Irvin. Sanders started at receiver in his place. Even though expectations remained high after the third Super Bowl title, it was just bad from the start.

Tight end Jay Novacek suffered a season-ending injury.

The Cowboys, however, rebounded to go 8–3 after Irvin returned. They won the NFC East for the fifth straight year. But they did not secure a first-round bye in the playoffs.

Things looked to be back on track when they trashed the Minnesota Vikings, 40–15, in the wild card playoffs.

Fittingly, the week before the divisional playoffs began with more off-the-field controversy. False accusations against Irvin and tackle Erik Williams made the news. Television satellite trucks were camped at the practice facility, which distracted the team.

Then it all fell apart in a seemingly winnable game against the expansion-team Carolina Panthers.

On the Cowboys' first possession, Irvin was sidelined with a fractured collarbone.

Sanders was lost for the game with a concussion.

The Cowboys suffered three turnovers in a surprising 26–17 loss.

"No, I'm not shocked, but I am extremely disappointed, as I think everybody is," Troy said of the loss. "I think a lot of people didn't believe that they are a good team, and they are."

Jerry Jones was philosophical after the game, thinking it was just a bad day at the office, but he had hopes of more good days to come.

"I can't stand here and sing the blues, after all the good things that have happened to us," he said. "This was just not our day."

It was not only not the Cowboys' day. It was the true ending of the Cowboys' dynasty.

CHAPTER 12

THE VICTORY AGAINST THE VIKINGS was the last play-off win the Cowboys would see until the 2009 season.

Haley finally retired after the 1996 season.

The inability to bring in new talent continued to eat away at the core.

And Barry Switzer remained as loose on the reins as ever. This time, he made the news at the start of the season when he was arrested at the airport for having a gun in his bag.

To prove he was serious about rebuilding the Cowboys' tarnished image, Jerry Jones fined Switzer $75,000—the largest fine ever imposed on an NFL coach at the time. Switzer also ended up pleading guilty to a misdemeanor, with a judge ordering him to pay a $3,500 fine and perform eighty hours of community service.

Still, the Cowboys started well, winning three of their first four games. That included a 37-7 trouncing of the Pittsburgh Steelers in the opener and a 27-3 victory against the Chicago Bears in game four.

But all that glitters is not gold.

★ ★ ★

The Cowboys lost nine of their last twelve games to finish 6-10.

Emmitt Smith missed parts of five games with injuries, and fullback Daryl Johnston missed ten games with a neck injury.

It ended a streak of five straight division titles.

After a 20-7 loss to the Giants in the season finale, it seemed clear that a change needed to be made and that Switzer was going to be the fall guy.

"We're better than six and ten," Troy said. "This didn't happen overnight. This has been happening over a couple of years, and it all caught up to us. Some things need to be addressed.

"I have no idea what's going to happen, and it's not for me to decide," Troy added when he was asked if he was pointing to Switzer. "Jerry will make decisions on the best interest of this organization."

To his credit, Switzer himself suggested after the game that he should pay the ultimate price. He told the team that the woeful season, which had begun with his arrest, had been his fault.

"I'm personally responsible," Switzer said. "It starts with the head coach on down. It was an ugly performance. . . . I told Jerry after the game, he ought to get rid of the whole damn bunch of us. Jerry will make the decision, and we'll talk about that in the future. This is not the time or place to talk about it."

Jones took three weeks to decide, before Switzer decided for him, announcing his own resignation.

"At this time, I believe a fresh start at this position will give the Cowboys their greatest opportunity to return to the top," Switzer said in a statement.

"I am deeply proud of what our players and coaches have been able to accomplish. A Super Bowl championship and three division titles are a source of great pride for this organization and its fans."

Jones, still believing the Cowboys could return to the top, called the 1997 season a temporary setback.

He was going to find the right coach to work within his system in hopes of returning the fading Cowboys to their past glory while Troy, Irvin, and Smith were still in the prime of their careers.

"We have come to the realization we must chart a fresh and new path in returning this team to the level of success our fans demand . . . of being a Super Bowl team," Jones said.

Irvin certainly saw the frustration in Troy and understood why it ultimately didn't work with Switzer.

"For him, I can understand," Irvin said. "He was so directed and detailed. He didn't mind having fun. But be directed and detailed. And Jimmy fits that description. It was a lesser degree with Barry."

Much lesser.

★ ★ ★

Troy was initially reinvigorated by the thought of a coaching change, especially when it appeared that his former UCLA coach, Terry Donahue, was going to get the job.

Donahue met three times with Jones. He spent the night in Jones's mansion in Dallas. A news conference was even planned to introduce him as coach.

And then the deal came undone, partly because of the working environment Jones was setting up. In Jones's plan, the head coach would not hire his own assistants. Most incoming head coaches would prefer to name their own staff.

Another sticking point was a low salary and an "insubordination" clause in Donahue's contract. He would be fined $25,000 every time he said something negative about the Cowboys or Jones.

"We never thought that the insubordination clause, and certainly the money, would be the things that turned it one way or the other," Jones said. "He was offered the job.... I did feel he'd come in as a coordinator on an entry-level basis [pay scale] into the NFL as opposed to coming in as a Super Bowl coach."

It all proved to be a deal breaker for Donahue. He ultimately passed on the offer.

Troy is admittedly still bothered by how it all went down.

But Jones moved on.

It took six weeks before he named relatively unknown Pittsburgh Steelers offensive coordinator Chan Gailey as head coach. Gailey was given one of the lowest salaries of any coach in the NFL. He seemed to accept not being able to hire his own assistants.

He was hired to revamp the Cowboys' offense, which had grown old and stale. The offense had scored seventeen or fewer points in nine of those final twelve games in 1997.

But Gailey knew Jones was the ultimate decision-maker.

"Everyone knows the final decision goes through this gentleman right here," Gailey said as he pointed toward Jones at his opening news conference. "We're going to have a great working relationship, and we're going to make decisions in the best interest of this football team. It's not who's right but what's right for the team."

Gailey was a good coach, a respected offensive mind.

He was religious and principled.

So he was likable.

But he was also probably too nice for a team that was still used to the laid-back environment of the Barry Switzer era. As a result, he was seen as a puppet. Players circumvented him to go straight to Jerry Jones's office when they had a complaint.

It is well known that Gailey didn't like players with big personalities or big egos.

And because of Irvin's history of getting in trouble, Gailey led the draft charge in 1998 to avoid taking future Hall of Fame receiver Randy Moss, who went to the Minnesota Vikings. Moss was perceived as an off-the-field risk. So a team that was on the decline passed on a once-in-a-lifetime player, who some believe could have helped lift the Cowboys back to the Super Bowl glory that Jones and company so badly wanted.

Gailey drew the ire of Troy because he changed the offense to more of a short-passing game. He tried to make Irvin a slot receiver and then tried to bench him.

"We were going from an older team to a younger team," Gailey said. "We were trying to win in transition."

At first, it seemed to be working. The Cowboys scored thirty or more points in seven of their first twelve games. They finished with a 10–6 record and won the division for the sixth time in seven years.

The Cowboys won the division only because the rest of the teams were awful. Then they shockingly lost to the Arizona Cardinals in the wild card playoffs at home.

The Cardinals, who had lost to the Cowboys twice in the regular season, hadn't been to the playoffs since 1982. They'd last won a playoff game in 1947. Yet they dominated the Cowboys, 20–7, in a game that wasn't as close as the score suggests.

Aikman completed only twenty-two of forty-nine passes for 191 yards, and Smith ran for only seventy-four yards on sixteen carries.

Gailey's new offense fell flat.

Troy stormed to the sidelines after one series and shouted, "I can't find anyone open."

Cowboys wide receiver Patrick Jeffers said, "We felt they knew our routes before we ran them."

The trip to the playoffs proved to be more of a last hurrah for some aging champions than a major return to glory.

"We were asked a lot during the week, 'Is the window of opportunity closing?'" Troy said after the game. "For a lot of people, that window shut a long time ago. We don't have a lot of the players who were here when we had that success. We are looking through a different window right now."

Jones, however, remained undeterred in his belief that the Cowboys still had the talent to return to the Super Bowl.

He doubled down on Troy still being the future of the franchise by once again making him the highest-paid player in the NFL with an $85.5 million contract extension through 2007. The deal added six seasons to the three remaining on the quarterback's contract. Aikman received $13 million of it upon signing and would get the remaining $7 million in early 2001.

Jones also tried to help him out on offense by signing the speedy Raghib Ismail to join the receiver corps.

The 1999 season started off well, too. The Cowboys began with a 41–35 victory against the Washington Redskins. It was the biggest comeback of Troy's career. The Cowboys had trailed by twenty-one points in the fourth quarter before rallying to victory.

The game winner came in overtime with a seventy-six-yard touchdown pass to Ismail. It was Troy's club record–tying fifth touchdown pass of the game.

But even then there was a hint of dissension, because Irvin wasn't being used much in the game.

"I see Michael on the sideline, and I say, 'What's wrong with you? Why aren't you in the game?'" Troy recalled. "He says, 'I don't know.' I'm thinking, 'Well, we put Michael in the game, then we can start coming back.'"

In fact, it would never be the same for Irvin.

Three games later, against the Philadelphia Eagles, he caught a short pass and didn't get up after he was tackled.

The fans in Philadelphia derisively cheered as he was taken to a spine trauma center.

"It was a compliment for Philly to cheer me," Irvin said. "Philly wasn't cheering my injury. They were cheering my departure. 'Thank God he's leaving the field; he's been killing us. Thank God, maybe now we have a chance to win.'"

Michael Irvin would never catch another pass from Troy Aikman. He would never play again.

The injury was initially diagnosed as swelling between two vertebrae in Irvin's neck. But doctors discovered a narrowing of the spine that could potentially lead to paralysis if he were to sustain a similar hit again.

The Cowboys lost that game to the Eagles, and then they lost three of their next four games.

The only highlight was a victory against the Jimmy Johnson–led Miami Dolphins on Thanksgiving Day.

"It was different for Jimmy Johnson to be here, and it was important for our team and fans to come out and get a nice win," giddy owner Jerry Jones said. "Yes, I am happy."

The Cowboys finished 8–8 and landed a wild card playoff spot. However, they were blown out,

27–10, by the Minnesota Vikings and receiver Randy Moss—the man Gailey had refused to draft the year before.

It would prove to be the end of the era, the end of the decade, and the end for Chan Gailey.

The Cowboys were undoubtedly the team of the 1990s, with three Super Bowl titles. And Troy won ninety games in the nineties, which at the time was more than any quarterback in NFL history in any decade.

Troy never publicly came out against Gailey.

But it was no secret that he was unhappy with the offense.

He was the highest-paid player in the NFL, and Gailey was the lowest-paid coach. Jerry Jones ultimately decided that Aikman had not been given a chance to succeed and that a change was necessary.

Jones felt Gailey's approach did not play to the strengths of Troy or running back Emmitt Smith.

The strong-armed quarterback was frustrated by having to throw too many dump-off passes. Smith's misuse was symbolized by the Cowboys' going 4–5 in 1999 in games in which he rushed for one hundred yards. The Cowboys had gone 53–9 in such games the previous nine years.

"I couldn't read what was going on with him and Chan," Irvin said. "I was fighting with what was going on with Chan and myself. The short-passing game wasn't suitable for his great talent. He whizzed the eight route, and now we [were] going to have him drop off all those short balls. That was crazy. I thought Troy did what he did with it. You had an offense [that] won you three Super Bowls. Now somebody else come[s] in with an offense that hasn't won you any."

The eight route is a combination of a seam and a post pattern or skinny post. The receiver runs about twelve yards straight downfield, then subtly breaks to an inside angle.

It was the bread-and-butter play for Troy and Michael during those Super Bowl years. But it was a relic in the team's offense under Gailey.

So Gailey, the only coach in Cowboys history to not win a Super Bowl, was fired.

The frustration of the decline and the way the Cowboys continued to go about things started to wear more and more on Troy. And it made it tougher for him to come to work and listen to Jones preach about how this was going to be the year.

"I would say, 'Okay, I'm going to be positive. I'm not going to let this get to me,'" Troy said. "And then, before I'd finish my first cup of coffee, you know, something would happen and I'm right back in that dark place."

Troy witnessed two other departures that hit closer to home. Fullback Daryl Johnston retired because of a neck injury, and Michael Irvin made his departure official a few months later.

Tests showed that Irvin was born with a narrow spinal cord, a condition that made him vulnerable to much more serious injury. He faced that risk every time he stepped onto a football field and never knew it.

The injury could have happened much earlier in his career, and he could have been paralyzed.

"Walking away from the game is hard, but walking away is a blessing," a teary-eyed Irvin said during his news conference.

Unbeknownst to many, Troy would make a similar speech roughly a year later.

CHAPTER 13

IN 2000, TROY AIKMAN trudged on with a new coach—Dave Campo, who had been promoted from defensive coordinator to replace Chan Gailey.

Campo was the last remaining member of Jimmy Johnson's original 1989 coaching staff still with the organization.

Jerry Jones also got Troy another shiny new toy to work with after Irvin's retirement. He traded two first-round picks to the Seattle Seahawks for speedy receiver Joey Galloway, who was then signed to a seven-year, $42 million contract.

Jerry Jones continued to feel that Troy was the backbone of the franchise, and getting him as many weapons as possible was the key to any hopes of their returning to the Super Bowl.

Ironically, Troy and Galloway would never make one connection together. The Campo era was dead on arrival.

It soured in the opening game of 2000 against the Philadelphia Eagles, in what is known as the Pickle Juice Game.

It was one of the hottest NFL games on record. To combat the 109-degree temperature at kickoff, the Eagles drank . . . pickle juice! It was supposed to prevent cramping and dehydration, and the Eagles players felt it gave them an edge in the game. Later, scientific studies would prove that drinking pickle juice really does help stop cramping.

Whether it was the pickle juice or not, the Eagles opened the game with an onside kick and ended up with a 41–14 blowout victory.

Aikman missed his first five passes. Then he suffered a concussion, his second in eleven games dating to 1999. He had to leave the game early.

Galloway sustained a season-ending knee injury in the fourth quarter.

The Cowboys finished the season 5–11, the first of three straight 5–11 seasons under Campo.

But the story of the season happened in a 32–13 victory against the Washington Redskins on December 10.

★ ★ ★

It was a third and goal from the 1, and Troy rolled to his right before being slammed to the turf by Redskins linebacker LaVar Arrington.

He suffered another concussion as well as jarring his back.

It would prove to be the last play of Troy's career.

He sat out the final two games, including a 31–0 blowout by the Tennessee Titans on Christmas Day.

After the season, decisions had to be made by Jones and Troy, who initially didn't want to retire. Troy had a degenerative back condition and had suffered twelve concussions in his career, including four in 1999 and 2000.

So on March 7, 2001, the day before Jones would

have to pay Troy a $7 million bonus, he cut the first player he'd ever drafted, the only quarterback he had ever known, and the one who had led him to three Super Bowl titles.

"This has been a difficult day personally, and one of the most difficult in my twelve years of being associated with the Cowboys," Jones said at a news conference at the club's Valley Ranch training complex that day. "A lot of people in this organization will be sad that Troy is not playing. But if you're in my shoes and you've been able to wake up with a franchise quarterback for the last twelve years, that's a luxury. I'm going to miss that.

"Troy will always be a Dallas Cowboy. When people look at him, they will always see him with a star on the side of his helmet."

Troy was just thirty-four, and he wasn't quite sure he was ready to walk away from the game, but he knew his time with the Cowboys had to come to an end.

"Retirement is a viable option, but based on the fact that I'd like to continue to play, that will be down the road," Troy said. "It's a matter of finding a situation I can be comfortable in and still play the game that I have a desire to play. I'm still capable of playing at a high level and remaining healthy."

Former offensive coordinator Norv Turner had been hired as the offensive coordinator for the San Diego Chargers, so reuniting with him was one of the options on the table.

The Chargers needed a quarterback, and Troy was familiar with the system.

"I obviously have a lot of respect for Norv, so that would certainly be a positive," Troy said. "Time will tell, if it's something I'm interested in and something that can be worked out.

"As far as saying without a shadow of a doubt that I'll be playing football in the 2001 season—I can't say that."

Roughly a month later, in a tear-filled news conference at Texas Stadium, Troy called it a career. In a ninety-minute news conference, the quarterback who had been unflappable on the field was overcome with emotion throughout.

Jones presented a video prepared by NFL Films

at the beginning. There were clips of a young Troy, and it featured great highlights of his career.

"You watch, and you think your time will never come," Troy said slowly, while dabbing under his eyes. "And my time's come.

"I know it's the right thing for me because of my health, concussions, the back problems I've had," Troy added. "It took its toll."

Troy took pride in remembering the team's transformation from 1–15 in 1989 and his own 0–11 record as a rookie to the pinnacle of it all with three Super Bowl titles in four years.

He said he cherished the character of the teammates who had helped make the Cowboys the dynasty team of the 1990s.

But he also displayed the candor and honesty that he'd been raised with.

"The chemistry of that ball club and unselfish manner—you can't beat that combination," he said. "Maybe over recent years, we've lost sight of that. It's become a game of players showcasing themselves."

Troy told Jerry Jones upon his retirement that

as much as he enjoyed the early part of his career and the success of the Cowboys, the final years were equally frustrating.

"Everything we had done to be successful during the Super Bowl years, we were no longer doing on a consistent basis," Troy said. "My disappointment was that we weren't giving ourselves a chance by doing the necessary things to be successful. . . . Those were some good years for me and for others that we kind of pushed away because of bad decisions."

It wasn't just about the loss of Jimmy Johnson and the lack of discipline that came with Barry Switzer; it was also the talent drain and personnel decisions from the top on down that ate away at his joy for the game.

He says now he could have and would have played two more years if the environment had been right.

"I just finally had enough. I just said, 'I can't do it anymore,'" Troy said. "I was prepared to sign with San Diego, but they signed Doug Flutie. So then I retired. If the situation was different, if we'd been doing things the right way and I was happy about it, I would have played another two or three years. And I would have played better. So the last play, I guess the last snap that I had, I did not know that that was going to be it for me."

Jason Garrett was the Cowboys' longtime backup quarterback and one of Troy's closest friends. (Now he's the Cowboys' head coach.) He witnessed the frustration up close.

"Troy was as good a football player as I have ever been around, as good a leader as I have ever been around," Garrett said. "The standard he had for himself and everybody else was really high. And after the first couple of years of his career, he had a stretch that was unlike many quarterbacks in the history of the NFL. Three Super Bowls in four years. So that became a standard for him.

"And when we were short of that, he was certainly frustrated at not being able to maintain that level. That was his greatness. Demanding first and foremost of himself and everybody around him to play to that level. I think that is where the frustration came from. He was a great football player. But that is the reason he was a great football player. He was a great leader. That is the reason he was a great leader. He wanted us to be the absolute best, championship standards in everything we did."

CHAPTER 14

TROY DIDN'T EXPECT TO quit football in 2001 at the age of thirty-four, but he did have another career waiting for him. It proved to be a surprise to many: television.

As quarterback of the Cowboys, Troy was intentionally stale during news conferences. It was his job to be the leader and the voice of the team. He purposely avoided showing a lot of personality. He believed quarterbacks must always be even-keeled and show a certain amount of confidence and calmness in the face of adversity.

"My locker ... was right next to his, and to see how he talked to the media every day and how he always put the team first," Garrett said. "It was never about him. It was always about the team. It was always about winning. It was always about doing things the right way. That is what he thought was the most important thing. That is the way he lived every single day."

So it's no accident that Garrett has made it a point to use his former teammate as an example when talking to current Cowboys quarterback Dak Prescott on how to carry himself and interact with the media.

"He is a great example," Garrett said of Troy. "He is one of the greatest players who ever walked. A lot of it has to do with his ability. A lot of it has to do with his approach. He walks into the room. He commands the room, commands the huddle. He doesn't suffer fools wisely. He just locks in on what he needs to do, and everyone followed. That is what you are trying to instill."

Still, it proved to be somewhat of a shock when Fox Sports hired Troy as an NFL game analyst in 2001.

It came as a result of a lark of sorts. Troy had

done a series of games in NFL Europe with Cowboys play-by-play voice Brad Sham in 1998 and 2000.

Troy thought it would be a good opportunity to get a free vacation to Europe.

But he proved to be better than expected and was soon offered a job by Fox.

He went from sharing a booth as a color analyst with former teammate Daryl Johnston to being promoted to the number one color analyst after the departure from Fox of the legendary John Madden in 2002.

He has not only been an excellent announcer, earning three Emmy nominations, but he has also been funny and refreshing.

Garrett didn't know Aikman was headed toward broadcasting after his career, but he is not surprised with Troy's success.

"He is one of the great storytellers and most enjoyable people I have known to be around," Garrett said. "He has great friends. He is a great friend. He is a special guy. We all knew he had a great personality. I didn't know he had an interest in going into broadcasting. Doesn't surprise me one bit how well he has done. One of the hardest-working and most-prepared people I have ever been around. That is how he approaches his job now."

Michael Irvin said it was a misconception that Troy was all business and didn't have any fun with his teammates in the locker room. Still, he didn't see television in his future.

"He was fun and funny," Irvin said. "Don't fool yourself. He was fun. . . . I didn't see him doing what he is doing now. Nobody did. If anybody tells you they did, they are lying. And then to be as good as he is. He is the best out there doing it. He is the best out there."

Babe Laufenberg, a former Cowboys backup quarterback and one of Aikman's closest friends, said he could foresee Troy's natural talent as an analyst even when he was a player. But Laufenberg didn't know Aikman would become among the best in the business.

"I knew Troy could do it," Laufenberg said. "It's hard to project someone doing it and then going to the top of the profession. So, to say he is going to be the best—and you can make the argument that he is the best analyst or certainly in the discussion—a lot of things probably go into that. I did know this: I knew he had a great personality."

Laufenberg said what people didn't understand is that Aikman was often answering questions for other people, whether it was on the Jerry-Jimmy situation, Switzer, or Irvin's issues. Troy was rarely talking about himself. He was talking about issues surrounding the organization. So naturally he would be guarded.

"He was almost like the coach, where the coach gets up there and really doesn't say anything," Laufenberg said. "But I knew he had a lot to say, and he had a lot of personality."

The other thing Laufenberg said he knew is that Aikman was going to approach his job as he did working on the farm for his dad and his football career.

"Whatever he decided to do, he was going to work his rear end off," Laufenberg said. "You don't get there and stay there if you're not good. I always say that job is a little bit like opening a restaurant, because your name is on it. You are Troy Aikman.

People are going to go. But if the food is not good and the service is not good, they are not coming back. He obviously had a great entrée. People like Dallas Cowboys quarterbacks. They like three-time Super Bowl winners. They like Super Bowl MVPs in the broadcast world. They got his foot in the door, and he keeps his foot in the door because he is really good and works really hard."

The work ethic is who he is and who he has always been.

Being a quarterback, let alone the quarterback of the Cowboys, was a great foundation for his career as a broadcaster. Quarterbacks have a great perspective on it because they see the big picture.

"You are not just responsible to yourself. You are responsible to the offense, the defense, the coaching staff," said Laufenberg, who is the analyst for the Cowboys radio broadcast. "Many times between the coaching staff and players, you have the head coach's ear. You've got this great overall view of the entire organization. When you bring that to the broadcast booth, you have a great understanding."

Aikman studies game tape for his broadcasts

as he did as a player. The Cowboys provide him as much game tape as he needs, no matter the team.

"I dig down pretty deep," Aikman told the *Los Angeles Times*. "There's a lot to look at—players, scheme, personnel. You start studying a particular guy and then it's, what personnel groupings are they using? Then you go back and look at it a little bit differently and try to figure out what exactly they're trying to accomplish. When I was playing, I wasn't worried about [watching] defensive linemen. That's somebody else's job to plot those guys. I'd study coverages, study blitzes, and I'd study one team, one defense for that week. Now it's four times as much film, both sides of the ball for two teams."

Aikman doesn't waste players' and coaches' time with chitchat and small talk just as he didn't like his time wasted when broadcasters came to talk to him while he was preparing for a game.

Aikman recalled an instance to the *Los Angeles Times* when an analyst tried to small-talk him before a game when he was playing.

"I said, 'Listen, if you want to know how I'm doing, I'll get up and leave right now,'" Aikman said. "If you want to know about the game, I'm happy to talk about the game. But we're not going to sit here and small-talk, and [ask] 'How's life?' and 'How's the family?'

"You try to be respectful of guys' time," he said. "This is, in a way, an inconvenience for them. So I try to be mindful of that."

That story doesn't surprise Laufenberg. He said Aikman remains the same guy he has always been. "My guess, if you knew him when he was twelve, he is the same guy. No nonsense. He doesn't suffer fools gladly. He wants to be in and out. If you tell him, 'I need you for ten minutes,' he will give you ten minutes. He will be on time if the ten minutes are up. He will say, 'I gave you ten minutes.' The beauty of Troy is you know exactly what you are getting. That personality at seventeen is the same as it is today."

★ ★ ★

There was only one time when Aikman really considered returning to the game.

It came in 2002, when he was working a game for Fox. He just so happened to see that Philadelphia

Eagles quarterback Donovan McNabb broke his ankle during a game. Then at halftime, Troy got a call from Eagles coach Andy Reid, who asked him to come out of retirement in time for the game the following week.

He said he would call Reid after his broadcast, while he was driving from San Diego, where he was working the game, to his home in Santa Barbara.

He then told Reid he wanted to sleep on it.

"So I went to bed that night and said, 'I can wake up tomorrow and spend a nice couple of days in Santa Barbara. Or I can be in frigid Philadelphia getting my brains kicked in,'" Aikman said when recalling the story in 2009.

He called Reid the following morning to give him the bad news.

As of this writing, he is in year eighteen of his broadcasting career and has never looked back.

★ PERSONAL LIFE ★

In the years since his retirement, Troy Aikman has had a few beginnings off the field.

In September 2017, he got married for a second time. Less than nine months later, he opened the aptly named Troy's, a restaurant at Texas Live!—a dining and entertainment complex at the Texas Rangers' Globe Life Park.

"It's inspired by a lot of the great Texas beer halls," Aikman told reporters. "I've been thinking for a while about jumping in and opening a restaurant, having something that I can put my name on, and this is a great opportunity for me."

Aikman helped design and come up with the menu for Troy's. There's live music indoors and outdoors, a beer garden, and, of course, big-screen TVs.

"You can't have a restaurant with my name on it and not have big screens for watching games," Aikman told reporters. "Especially games where I'm broadcasting."

Troy's serves mainly gourmet burgers and bar food. But it also has some nice appetizers, including an artichoke dip using his wife's recipe.

It's the perfect touch, because Troy Aikman

wouldn't be involved in the restaurant, nor would he have accepted an additional Thursday night broadcast assignment that has him doing two games a week with Fox Sports, if not for the support of his wife, Capa Aikman.

After a courtship of little more than a year, Aikman proposed in June 2017. And the usually private former football star was so happy and joyful that he announced the engagement via social media, sharing a photo of the couple on a romantic outing on a boat in Lake Como, Italy. He captioned the photo "June 2, 2017—a special day as I proposed to the love of my life."

On September 2, 2017, the two were married in Santa Barbara in a private beachside ceremony before family and close friends. It created a blended family that Troy said has made his life complete. He has two teenage daughters—Alexa Marie and Jordan Ashley—from a previous marriage, and Capa has two teenage sons, Luke and Val, from a previous marriage.

When he is not doing games for Fox, he is at

home with his family. He takes a private jet to his Thursday games and returns the same night. And he doesn't leave for his Sunday games until Saturday.

"It's afforded me the opportunity to be home on the weekend," Aikman said. "My stepson is playing on the varsity football team, and to be able to go watch his games—that has been nice."

And when he goes to the games, whether it's his son's football games or his daughter's volleyball games, he is in the stands, as far away as he can get, cheering and being supportive.

"I like being Dad and watching a game and being as far away from everybody as I can," said Aikman. He doesn't like parents who coach from the stands and are overly critical on every play.

He also learned long ago that he is too competitive to be a youth coach himself.

"I coached the girls as an assistant coach in a couple of sports, and I was way too competitive for that," Troy told *GQ* in the past. "I had the girls running sprints one day. One girl, she was playing . . . in the back of the line. She was probably six. I said, 'If you want to goof around, there's a playground over there.' . . . I knew my girls would see me in an entirely different light, and I just didn't want that. . . . I just want to be Dad."

Aikman said he never wanted to damage his relationship with his daughters. And they know him as Dad, rather than some big-time football player. They have never really asked much about his career. They know he is in the Hall of Fame and won Super Bowls. But they don't talk about it a lot.

He said he never tried to interject his experiences as a player into their life.

But he was appreciative over the last year when his younger daughter reached out to him about the anxiety of being a freshman on the varsity volleyball team, not wanting to make mistakes and disappoint the seniors.

"She said, 'Dad when you play and you make a mistake, you know, how would you get over that? Because I make a mistake, and it makes me make more mistakes. And so, I'm just wondering if you have any tips for me from back when you played,'" Aikman recalled.

"It really kind of, like, wow—it kind of hit me in a really soft spot. I've never been asked that by the girls."

Aikman said he also never believed in pushing his kids into doing something they don't want to do, an attitude he says he got from his father.

His daughter plays volleyball for her school but doesn't want to play club volleyball outside of school. Her high school coach would prefer that she did and asked Aikman to intercede.

He politely declined.

"She's going to do what she wants to do," Aikman said. "She's a good kid. She likes sports. She's doing well in school, and I'm happy for all the things she's doing.

"I tell my kids they're going to do three things

when they play. They're going to listen; they're going to do what Coach tells them. They're going to give great effort, and they're going to show good sportsmanship. And I say, 'If you do those three things, which you can do ... every game, you can do those things ... you, we, won't ever have a problem. I won't ever get on you about any of it.'"

It's no different from what he asked of his Cowboys teammates during his career.

★ ★ ★

Troy's amazing football career officially reached its final resting place in 2006, when he was named to the Pro Football Hall of Fame.

Troy was a no-brainer for the Hall of Fame as quarterback of three Super Bowl teams in four years and the team of the nineties.

He closed his career with ninety-four regular-season wins, including ninety in the 1990s, making him the winningest starting quarterback of any decade when he retired. He held or tied forty-seven Dallas passing records, including career attempts (4,715), completions (2,898), passing yards (32,942), touchdowns (165), and completion percentage (61.5) when he retired. And he was picked for six Pro Bowls.

But although he was the first overall pick in 1989 and predicted for greatness, his individual numbers paled in comparison with other top quarterbacks.

His story and career were never about individual greatness. It was always about hard work, leadership, sacrifice, and unselfish play for the good of the team.

He eloquently pointed that out upon his induction. The Hall of Fame was the only individual award that mattered.

"In Dallas, my role as the quarterback was to move our team down the field and score points," Troy said in his Hall of Fame speech. "Sometimes that meant passing the ball; sometimes it meant handing it off. We had a good system in Dallas. Although it wasn't one that allowed me to put up big numbers, that was fine. I did what was asked to help the team win. So it is extremely gratifying that after a career of putting team accomplishments in front of personal achievement, today I am receiving the greatest individual honor a football player could ever receive."

Troy never complained about the team's run-oriented offense, which allowed Emmitt Smith to become the league's all-time leading rusher, and he didn't allow his dislike for Switzer to prevent him from doing what was necessary to win the Super Bowl for the final time in 1996.

It's also true that Troy was at his best in the moments when the Cowboys were at their greatest.

"I was able to live a dream," Troy said. "I played professional football. That I was able to do so with so many great players and coaches and win three world championships and wind up here . . . it's almost too much to believe."

But it wasn't too much to believe if you understood where he came from and how he got there, starting in Cerritos, California, before putting down roots in Henryetta, Oklahoma.

Troy pointed out the sacrifices his mother, Charlyn, made to get him and his two sisters to practices and games, and always being there when they needed her.

He thanked his father, Kenneth, for teaching him the hard work, discipline, and toughness that would serve him well through his college days at Oklahoma and UCLA and certainly in the NFL with the Cowboys. "My intensity on the field was a reflection of you, and your impact on my athletic career was greater than you'll ever know," Troy said.

The question now is: Where does Troy go from here?

He has enjoyed his post-football life as an NFL analyst and doesn't plan to leave anytime soon. But he said this is not his final role. He does have an inkling, make that an itch, to get back into football one day as a general manager.

He's found that there is a huge difference between playing the game and talking the game. He would like to be part of the inner workings of a franchise, similar to Hall of Fame quarterback John Elway, who is the general manager of the Denver Broncos.

"I don't think I'm in the role I will ultimately be in. I think there's more for me," Troy said. "This job with Fox has been great. One of the first Super Bowls I did was the Giants beating the Patriots with the [David] Tyree helmet catch. I was having dinner after the game and [Ron] Jaworski was talking about how great the game was. I said, 'Yeah, it was pretty good.' He asks me what's wrong. I say nothing, and he asks me why I'm not more excited. Well, I've won these, and I know what it feels like, but I didn't do anything. I just talked about it. I remember thinking to myself that night that this may be the most meaningful game I broadcast, and if I feel this empty, I'm in the wrong profession. It was a bit depressing.

"It was the last time I felt that way. I don't know what changed. Now I feel some fulfillment. I feel accomplishment following the games. Broadcasting has afforded me a great life to raise my daughters in. I'm at home during the week and some weekends. Front-office work is something I would be interested in, but I couldn't commit the time to that with young daughters. When they grow up, I still think there's something left for me to do that has maybe been in the back of my mind a long time. We'll see if an opportunity presents itself."

Troy said he may discuss the situation with Jerry Jones one day but understands that the Cowboys franchise is a family-oriented business, and the opportunity to do what he wants doesn't exist there.

And then there is the matter of trying to start something new after the age of fifty. He doesn't know how many opportunities there are for someone of his age to start fresh in a front office, though the hiring of former Tampa Bay safety John Lynch by the San Francisco 49ers in 2017 gives him some hope. Lynch went from the broadcast booth to the general manager's job.

Whenever Troy walks away from broadcasting, if he somehow doesn't land a front-office job in the NFL, look for him to walk from the public eye for good.

He will still do charity work. But his life as a celebrity will be over.

Charity work has always been important to Aikman. He established the Troy Aikman Foundation for children in 1992. It created colorful, interactive playrooms in children's hospitals called Aikman's End Zones. They featured cutting-edge home theaters and computers networked with other children's hospitals.

It was one of the reasons he was named the Walter Payton NFL Man of the Year in 1997.

Through the years, he also had a steady relationship with the United Way, appearing in commercials as a player and serving on its board after retirement.

In 2017, he dissolved his foundation and transferred its $1 million in assets to the United Way of Metropolitan Dallas's Unite Forever Campaign. That campaign, an effort announced last year to support North Texas education, health, and financial stability, has raised more than $35 million so far toward its $100 million goal.

He also established the Troy Aikman Foundation Fund in the United Way Foundation of Metropolitan Dallas—the first donor-advised fund for United Way of Metropolitan Dallas. He retains advisory privileges over the distribution and investment of the assets. He is also their signature spokesman for their yearly fund-raising campaigns.

"If broadcasting is my last step, and I officially retire [in] ten years or whatever it ends up being, I believe when I leave, I'll be gone from public life," Troy said. "Celebrity was never my motivation for doing anything. I've enjoyed whatever notoriety I have gotten because of success, but there will come a time I step away from all of it and be done. I'll still be in the community, but you won't be hearing a lot from me."

Aikman remains a living legend.

But his is a story that looks great in a package, all wrapped in a bow, that doesn't tell the hard work, setbacks, perseverance, and courage it took to achieve greatness.

Heck, he signed up for football in junior high only at the urging of his father.

He started his college career at the University of Oklahoma but suffered a broken leg in the fourth game of his sophomore season. Troy then watched his backup lead the team to the national title and become the Oklahoma hero that he had hoped to be.

He transferred to UCLA and finally became the best quarterback in college football. That set the stage for him to be drafted number one overall by the Dallas Cowboys.

But there was no perfect transition. The Cowboys went 1–15 his rookie season. Aikman had no relationship with Coach Johnson his first four years, and when the Cowboys finally made the playoffs in 1991, he had to watch his understudy take snaps in the first game because of an injury and broken promise. It felt like Oklahoma all over again.

The championships and success finally came with Super Bowl titles in 1993, 1994, and 1996.

A back injury eventually forced Aikman out of the game before the 2001 season, but the joy of the sport had already waned for a perfectionist who approached every game and every practice with the seriousness of his welder father. Aikman's parents taught him that it was not just important to do things right but it's also important to do the right things.

That was often in stark contrast to the environment of the Cowboys, who were as notorious off the field as they were flashy and showy on it.

But Aikman was the ultimate teammate through it all. He has long refused to go into detail about his teammates and their travails.

That leadership and responsibility, which he learned growing up in Henryetta, never waned.

"The person that I ultimately have become, things that helped me do some things I've done athletically, were really shaped in [Henryetta]," Aikman said. "I learned about hard work. I learned about integrity. I learned about character. I learned about your word meaning something.

"In the process of all that, it was supported by this wonderful community. I've said many times, I wish that every child had an opportunity to really experience what I got to experience in a small town."

It proved to be the foundation for his induction into the Pro Football Hall of Fame. It was never about yards, touchdowns, or accolades for him. It was about wins.

Besides his three Super Bowl titles, no quarterback ever had more wins in any decade than his ninety in the 1990s until Peyton Manning surpassed him in the following decade with 115 wins. Fittingly, like Troy, Manning was a number one overall pick and can't-miss prospect.

But it's never that easy.

"I think from the outside, it always looks like, 'Oh man. This guy just decides he's going to do this and off he went. He did it. What a great life he's had,'" Troy said with a smile.

"Well, I think everyone has those moments. You know, some more than others—and some more tragic than others, but I think everyone has setbacks. And kind of how you deal with those things is ultimately what determines whether or not you'll go forward and succeed or not. Not to be cliché, but I really have felt like the various setbacks that I've had have kind of paved the way for something better."

There is nothing better in football than winning Super Bowls and being inducted into the Pro Football Hall of Fame. There is nothing better in life than having a job you love and being surrounded by a loving family.

Troy Aikman, who doesn't talk much about his football career anymore, is living his best life now.

AUTHOR'S NOTE ON SOURCES

I am a sportswriter for the *Fort Worth Star-Telegram,* and I've been reporting on the Dallas Cowboys since 1996. I covered Troy Aikman's departure from the Cowboys, his retirement press conferences, and his induction into the Pro Football Hall of Fame. I interviewed Aikman for this book. I have also used quotes from personal interviews with Troy Aikman's mother, Charlyn Aikman; his agent, Leigh Steinberg; his childhood friend Daren Lesley; and his former teammates Michael Irvin, Babe Laufenberg, and Jason Garrett.

In addition, I relied on information from these sources: ESPN.com, NFL.com, *D* magazine, the Dallas

AUTHOR'S NOTE ON SOURCES

Cowboys media guides, and the online archives of the *Dallas Morning News,* the *Fort Worth Star-Telegram,* the *Los Angeles Times,* the *New York Times, Texas Monthly, Tulsa World,* the *Daily Oklahoman,* PBS, and the *Washington Post.*

Finally, the following books were helpful sources:

Aron, Jaime. *Dallas Cowboys: The Complete Illustrated History.* Minneapolis: MVP Books, 2010.

Housewright, Ed. *Dallas Cowboys America's Team: Celebrating 50 years of Championship NFL Football.* New York: Associated Press, 2010.

Pearlman, Jeff. *Boys Will Be Boys.* New York: Harper Collins, 2008.

Taylor, Jean-Jacques. *Game of My Life Dallas Cowboys: Memorable Stories from Cowboys Football.* Champaign, IL: Sports Publishing LLC, 2006.

Thomas, David. *Dallas Cowboys in the Hall of Fame.* Lanham, MD: Rowman & Littlefield, 2016.

INDEX

INDEX

INDEX

INDEX

INDEX

INDEX

INDEX

INDEX

DON'T MISS THESE
★ GAME FOR LIFE ★
BIOGRAPHIES!

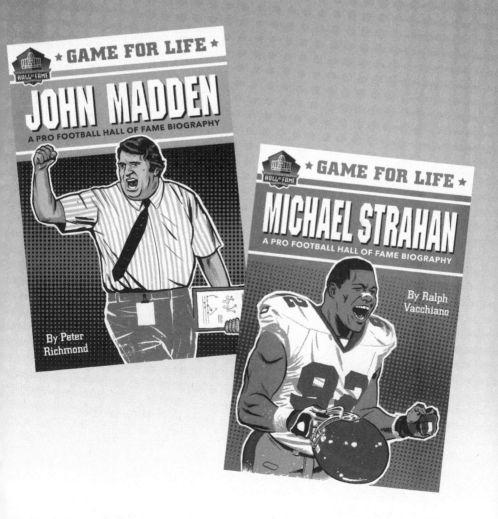